cool cake toppers

cool cake toppers

Put Anything You Want On A Cake

AMANDA RAWLINS AND CAROLINE DEASY

FIREFLY BOOKS

A FIREFLY BOOK

Published by Firefly Books Ltd., 2012

First Printing

Publisher Cataloging-in-Publication Data (U.S.)

Rawlins, Amanda, 1971-
     Cool cake toppers : put anything you want on a cake / Amanda Rawlins and Caroline Deasy.
Includes index.
ISBN 978-1-77085-038-5
     1. Cake decorating. 2. Sugar art. I. Deasy, Caroline, 1973- II. Title.
TX771.2.R39 2012   641.86'539   C2011-907908-9

Published in the United States by
Firefly Books (U.S.) Inc.
P.O. Box 1338, Ellicott Station
Buffalo, New York 14205

Published in Canada by
Firefly Books Ltd.
66 Leek Crescent
Richmond Hill, Ontario L4B 1H1

Printed in China

This book was conceived, designed, and produced by
Quintet Publishing Limited
6 Blundell Street
London N7 9BH

Project Editor: Lindsay Kaubi
Designer: Bonnie Bryan
Photographer: Tim Bowden
Pre Press: Gareth Butterworth
Editorial Director: Donna Gregory
Art Director: Michael Charles
Publisher: Mark Searle

Contents

Introduction   7

Tools and equipment   8

Baking the cake   10

Frosting   13

Fondant   16

Decorations   20

Directory of cake toppers 24

Buttons the bear	26
Baby cakes	28
Spotty duck	30
Baby name blocks	32
Nautical name cake	34
Enchanted garden	38
Verity the fairy	40
Digger, tractor and fire engine	42
Bobo the clown	44
Farm	46
Pirate treasure island	51
Cute cupcake toppers	54
Cute cupcake characters	56
Darcy, dog in a handbag	58
Princess	60
Boys' toys	62
Army	64
Quirky characters	66
Cool dudes	68

Rock tattoo	70
Girls' night in	72
Hippie chick	74
Movie night	78
Soccer field	80
Surf's up! Radical cakes	82
Pizza	86
Southern-fried chicken	88
Golf course	90
DIY	92
Garden	94
Shopping	98
Luau dancer	103
Fruit basket	106
Sunflower bouquet	110
Hobbies and occasions	112
Celebrations and thank yous	114
Casino night	116

Red, white and blue stars	118
Easter	120
Halloween	122
Christmas	124
Holiday wreath	126
Elves and stockings	128
Festive tree	130
Hydrangea centerpiece	132
Mini rose bouquet	134
Daisy cupcake tower	136
Wedding cupcakes	138

Templates	140
Index	142
Suppliers and credits	144

Introduction

As sisters, we have always shared a love of baking, since the days we baked jam tarts with our Mum. Over the years we have wowed our family and friends with our exquisite baked treats. That was until Mandy, while living in the U.S., discovered a passion for all things cupcake; she was amazed by how these little treasures could be transformed into objects of celebration in their own right.

On Mandy's return to the U.K., we decided to turn our hobby into a business, and cupcakeoccasions.co.uk was born. Cupcake Occasions has now flourished into an internationally recognized "cupcakery," with our handmade decorations now considered an art form. We are passionate about cake decorating and relish the next cupcake experience to get our teeth into: we are both continually challenging ourselves and the boundaries of cake decoration.

We have always felt that our craft is something that can be easily taught and are surprised every time by the excitement cake decoration evokes in people, especially the achievement of producing something beautiful when you think you have no skill!

This book aims to show that making your own *Cool Cake Toppers* is very achievable!

Every baker wants to personalize their celebration cakes, and *Cool Cake Toppers* will provide ideas and guidance to the amateur cake maker as well as inspiration to the professional.

Sharing our experience and the philosophy of "we can put anything on a cupcake," this book encourages everyone to create their own quirky cake toppers by:

- Providing a summary of the materials and equipment you will need to create your cake toppers.
- Showing the different effects that can be achieved within the sugar-craft realm, including the use of fondant, frosting techniques, coloring and edible and non-edible embellishments.
- Demonstrating step-by-step techniques that make it easy to produce professional-looking cake and cupcake toppers.

It's time to inspire the baker in you, awaken your inner artist and create something cool and amazing for your friends and family to delight over.

Enjoy!

Mandy and Caroline

Tools and equipment

The following equipment is recommended when baking either an 8-inch (20 cm) round cake, 12 cupcakes or 24 mini cupcakes.

BAKING EQUIPMENT

★ Cookie scoops: either 3 tablespoons (45 ml) for cupcakes or 1–1½ teaspoons (7 ml) for mini cupcakes (1)

★ Two 8-inch (20 cm) round baking pans (2)

★ 12-cup muffin pan or 24-mini-cup muffin pan (3)

★ Measuring spoons (4)

★ Cooling rack (5)

★ Cupcake liners: regular and mini sizes (6)

★ Parchment paper (7)

★ Cake board or drums that match your cake pan size

★ Stand mixer or handheld mixer

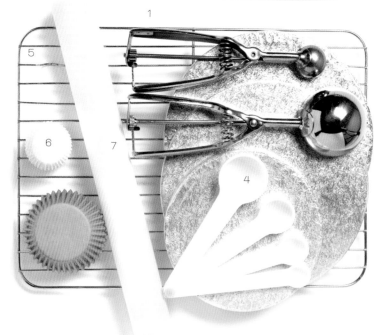

Here is a selection of the decorating tools used in this book. They are widely available from craft stores and other specialty stores. Although they are recommended, they are not essential, and you can find a multitude of alternatives in your kitchen; piping tips are perfect as small circle cutters and kitchen knives as blade tools.

DECORATING TOOLS

★ Piping bags (1)

★ Piping tips (2)

★ Rolling pin (3)

★ Cutters,
   various shapes (4)

★ Craft knife (5)

★ Spatula (6)

★ Modeling tools (7)

★ Toothpicks/wooden
   skewers (8)

★ Edible glue (9)

★ Paintbrushes (10)

★ Fondant smoother (11)

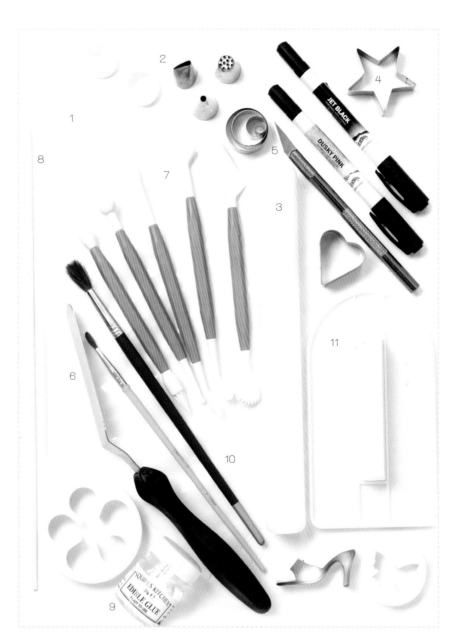

The following recipes for a vanilla sponge and a rich chocolate cake can be easily adapted to suit cakes or cupcakes. These recipes will yield enough batter for an 8-inch (20 cm) diameter cake or for 24 cupcakes. An 8-inch (20 cm) cake will feed between 12 and 15 people.

If you are not a confident baker, there is nothing wrong with using a store-bought cake mix. An 18¼ ounce (500 g) box will yield the same amount as the recipes listed here.

Ideally, the cake from this recipe should be eaten on the day it is baked, but the sponge will stay moist over-night if kept wrapped in plastic wrap. For a cake with a longer shelf life, we suggest using a store-bought cake mix because this will yield a sponge that can last up to five days. This is ideal for cakes that need to be made ahead, like celebration or wedding cakes. This recipe calls for the use of a stand mixer or handheld mixer.

VANILLA SPONGE

INGREDIENTS

10 ounces (285 g/1¼ cups/310 ml) butter, softened at room temperature

10 ounces (285 g/1½ cups/375 ml) superfine sugar

1 tsp (5ml) glycerine (optional, this helps keep the cake moist)

5 large eggs

1tsp vanilla extract

10 ounces (285 g/1½ cups/375 ml) cake flour

FOR VANILLA CAKE

★ Preheat the oven to 350°F (180°C) and line two 8-inch (20 cm) round cake pans with waxed paper.

★ Cream the butter, sugar and glycerine (if using) together until pale and fluffy. Beat in the eggs one at a time with a tablespoon (15 ml) of the flour and add in the vanilla extract. Mix until the ingredients are combined.

★ Add the remaining flour and beat until light and fluffy.

★ Divide between the two pans and bake for 40 minutes or until a skewer inserted into the middle of the cake comes out clean.

★ Leave to stand for 10 minutes and then turn onto a wire rack to cool.

FOR VANILLA CUPCAKES

★ Halve the above recipe to make twelve 2-inch (5 cm) cupcakes. Preheat the oven to 350°F (180°C) and lined cups a muffin pan with 12 muffin-sized cupcake liners. Use a tablespoon to evenly distribute the batter between the lined cups. To ensure even-sized cupcakes, you could use a 3-tablespoon (45 ml) sized cookie scoop. The batter should come half or two thirds of the way up the liners.

★ Bake for 17 to 20 minutes.

FOR MINI VANILLA CUPCAKES

★ Quarter the original recipe to make twenty-four 1¼-inch (3 cm) mini cupcakes. Preheat the oven to 350°F (180°C), and line a mini-muffin pan with 24 mini-muffin liners. Use a 1½-teaspoon (7 ml) cookie scoop to distribute the batter between the liners to ensure even-sized cupcakes.

★ Bake for 12 to 14 minutes.

RICH CHOCOLATE CAKE

INGREDIENTS

3½ ounces (100 g/¾ cup/175 ml)
cocoa powder

1½ cups (375 ml) of boiling water

6¾ ounces (190 g/⅞ cup/175 ml) butter,
softened at room temperature

14½ ounces (410 g/2 cups/500 ml)
superfine sugar

10½ ounces (300 g/2½ cups/625 ml)
all-purpose flour

¾ tsp (4 ml) baking soda

½ tsp (2 ml) baking powder

3 medium eggs

FOR RICH CHOCOLATE CAKE

★ Preheat the oven to 350°F (180°C).

★ Mix the cocoa powder with the boiling water and
allow to cool.

★ Line two 8-inch (20 cm) round cake pans with parchment paper.

★ Cream the butter and sugar together until pale and fluffy. Beat in
the eggs, one at a time, with a tablespoon (15 ml) of the flour to
avoid curdling. Mix until the ingredients are combined.

★ Add the remaining flour alternating with the cocoa mixture and then
fold in the remaining ingredients until combined. Divide between the
two pans and bake for 1 hour or until a skewer inserted into the
middle of the cake comes out clean.

★ Leave to stand for 10 minutes and then turn out onto a wire
rack to cool.

FOR RICH CHOCOLATE CUPCAKES

★ Halve the above recipe to make 12 cupcakes. Preheat the oven
to 350°F (180°C), and line a muffin pan with 12 muffin-sized
cupcake liners. Use a tablespoon or a 3-tablespoon (45 ml) sized
cookie scoop to distribute the batter between the liners. The
batter should come half or two thirds of the way up the liners.

★ Bake for 17 to 20 minutes.

FOR MINI RICH CHOCOLATE CUPCAKES

★ Quarter the original recipe to make 24 mini cupcakes.
Preheat the oven to 350°F (180°C), and line a mini-muffin
pan with 24 mini-muffin liners. Use a 1½ teaspoon (7 ml)
cookie scoop to distribute the batter between the liners to
ensure even-sized cupcakes.

★ Bake for 12 to 14 minutes.

Frosting

The following recipe will frost 24 cupcakes. You will need to halve this recipe to frost an 8-inch (20 cm) diameter cake in preparation for fondant covering.

FROSTING RECIPE

INGREDIENTS

5 ounces (140 g/¾ cup/175 ml) vegetable shortening

2½ ounces (70 g/⅓ cup/75 ml) unsalted butter, softened at room temperature

1 tsp (5 ml) glycerine (optional, this helps to keep the frosting light and fluffy)

1 tbsp clear vanilla essence

12 ounces (340 g/2¾ cups/675 ml) confectioners' sugar

2–3 tbsp (30–45 ml) of water

FOR MAKING FROSTING

★ Beat the vegetable shortening, butter, vanilla essence and glycerine (if using) until light and fluffy.

★ Add the confectioners' sugar and slowly incorporate with the other ingredients.

★ Add the water, turn up the mixer and beat on high for at least three minutes, until light and fluffy.

PREPARING A CAKE FOR FONDANT

★ Even out the cake by slicing any domed tops off both cakes. Sandwich the trimmed cakes together with frosting and seedless jelly, ensuring the bottom of the cake layer is facing up. You may need to trim the edges to remove any crust that may show through the fondant.

★ Place the cake on a cake board or drum 1-inch (2.5 cm) bigger than the cake. Cover the cake in a thin layer of frosting, but don't worry about creating a smooth, perfect finish. This acts as a glue for the fondant.

★ You can also place a table knife in a glass of freshly boiled water and skim the cake to provide an even surface.

★ Refrigerate the cake, preferably overnight, to firm up the cake and frosting.

COLORING FROSTING
AND BUTTERCREAM

★ Because buttercream is cream colored, you need to consider this when adding coloring. Using the whitest butter (unsalted butter) will result in a whiter buttercream.

★ Liquid food coloring is ideal for pastel shades, but it will not produce intense color.

★ To create intense colors you need to use color pastes. However, there is a warning! To obtain vibrant colors like red, black and purple, you will need to use lots of coloring to achieve the color you require, resulting in a runnier and bitter-tasting frosting/buttercream. The other side effect is that you may find that your guests are walking around with purple or black mouths after eating.

★ There are highly concentrated color pastes on the market that allow you to use less paste to produce a vibrant result.

FROSTING TECHNIQUES

These are the frosting techniques used for the designs in this book. A good tip is that it's much easier to place a piping bag in a drinking glass when filling it with frosting. No mess!

FROSTING A CUPCAKE WITH A WHIP

★ Fill a piping bag with the desired color of frosting and use a Wilton no.1M/2110 tip.

★ To swirl the top of the cupcake, start at the back of the cupcake, swirl around the edge and then continue inward to fill. Finally, release pressure and pull away.

★ Now pipe a smaller second ring in the center to form a peak.

★ Add any further decorations before the frosting sets.

HAND-PIPED ROSES

★ Fill the piping bag with the desired color of frosting and use a Wilton no. 104 petal tip.

★ You can either pipe onto a small piece of parchment paper on a piping nail and then transfer to the cake/cupcake after piping or you can pipe directly onto a cupcake.

★ Position the tip onto the center of the nail/cupcake, with the wide end touching the base. Apply pressure and turn the nail/cupcake a complete turn until you form a cone shape.

★ Start the first petal with the wide end of the tip touching the base of the cone, then turn the nail/cupcake and gently lift and drop to form the first petal.

★ Start the second petal a third of the way back and over the first petal. Repeat the same motions as for the first petal. You should aim to have three petals around the cone.

★ Continue the petal motion until you have completed the rose.

★ The same method applies to mini cupcakes.

GRASS OR HAIR

★ Color the frosting green, fill the piping bag, and use a Wilton no. 233 multi-opening tip.

★ Practice a few strokes by applying pressure to the cake and then pulling away to create grass.

★ The same method can be used to give the effect of hair.

MULTICOLORED FROSTING

★ This technique allows you to mix more than one frosting color and create some cool effects, such as fire—red, yellow and orange, and water—white and blue.

★ Place your piping bag with the desired tip in a drinking glass and fill each side with a different color of frosting. Squeeze the piping bag and practice a few strokes until the colors merge.

Fondant

Fondant is a sugar-based icing with a dough-like consistency, which is ideal for covering cakes and modeling cake decorations. It is readily available in supermarkets in white. More colors are available from specialty stores.
You can easily color white fondant with either food coloring or color pastes.
After use, if adequately wrapped, it will keep until its expiration date.

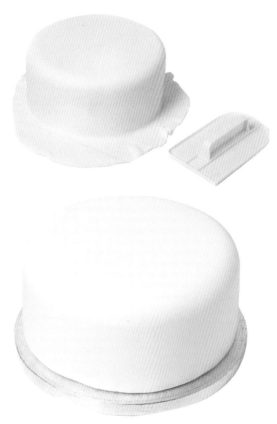

COVERING A CAKE IN FONDANT

★ After frosting the cake in a thin, rough layer (see page 13), take the cake out of the fridge 30 minutes before you plan to cover with fondant.

★ Lightly cover a flat surface with confectioners' sugar and roll out 15 ounces (425 g) of your desired color of fondant in a circular shape and to a thickness of ¼ inch (7 mm).

★ Lift the fondant over the cake to cover it and use your hands to gently smooth the fondant over the cake.

★ If there are any air bubbles, pop them with a pin and gently smooth them out with your finger.

★ Using a fondant smoother, start at the top of the cake and smooth the fondant to ensure a flat and even surface. Repeat on the sides of the cake. Trim any excess fondant with a knife.

★ Covering a cake in fondant keeps the sponge moist for up to a week after baking. This allows you to bake ahead and finish the cake decoration prior to a big event or occasion.

★ Allow to dry for 24 hours before decorating.

FLAT FONDANT-COVERED CUPCAKE

★ To achieve a smooth, flat fondant-covered cupcake, roll out the fondant as described at left and use a 2½-inch (6.5 cm) circle cutter to cut out a circle.

★ Apply 1 tablespoon (15 ml) of frosting to the top of the cupcake. Place the circle of fondant on top and smooth with the palm of your hand until flat.

COLORING FONDANT

You can easily color white fondant to your desired color by using either food coloring or color pastes.

For pastel shades, use a toothpick to dot the desired color into the fondant. Knead on a surface dusted with confectioners' sugar until you reach the desired shade. You may need to add more food coloring as you work.

Alternatively, if you have fondant in a primary color, you can mix a small amount of the colored fondant with white fondant to reach your desired shade.

It's just like mixing paint colors:
Pink = white + red
Lemon = white + yellow
Lilac = white + grape
Tan = white + brown or chocolate-flavored fondant

To mix stronger colors yourself, it's best to use coloring paste.

COLOR EFFECTS

The versatility of fondant allows you to mix a number of colors to create some exciting effects.

Water = white + pale blue + blue
Marble = white + small amount of black
Wood = brown + small amount of tan
Parchment = tan + small amount of brown

Roll the colors into equal length sausages and then roll together, bend in half and press together; repeat the process until you reach the desired effect. The key is not to over-mix the fondant to blend the colors. Roll out the fondant and use as directed.

MAKING CAKE AND CUPCAKE TOPPERS FROM FONDANT

Do you remember modeling dough when you were a child? Fondant is exactly the same! You can create almost anything from fondant. Fondant is ideal for cake decorations as it is pliable and is hard enough to support itself when dry.

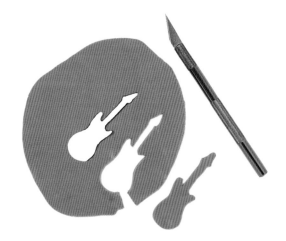

MODELING

To make the fondant pliable, knead it on a surface dusted with confectioners' sugar or cornstarch. You can then mold it or roll it out to cut out decorations freehanded or with cutters. For the decorations in this book you should roll the fondant to 1/16 inch (2 mm) thick unless otherwise directed.

TEMPLATES

A number of templates are supplied on pages 140–141. These can be photocopied and cut out with scissors. You can then place the template on the rolled fondant and cut around it with a craft knife. You can tidy the edges of your cutout with either the edge of the knife or your finger. If the recipe calls for a cutter that you do not have, you can always make your own template or try and cut it out freehanded.

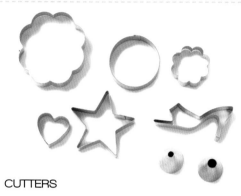

CUTTERS

There is a vast array of cutters available in both supermarkets and specialty stores, and you will probably already have a few in your kitchen drawers. You can also be imaginative with other tools and equipment you have in your kitchen; piping tips are perfect for small circles and drinking glasses for larger circles.

DRYING

Once you have made your decoration, lay it on parchment paper on a flat surface. Most decorations call for a 24-hour drying time, but many will probably support their own weight after just a few hours. Once dry, your decorations will keep for at least two weeks, which is ideal when you are creating a celebration cake and cupcakes and want to get ahead, instead of creating a masterpiece on the morning of the event!

FRILLING

Frilling is good for creating skirts, blankets and other fabrics. It is also used in the rosette (see page 118). Placing a skewer over the edge of the fondant where the taper of the skewer starts and gently rolling it along the fondant achieves this effect.

Decorations

There are many ways to embellish your cakes and cupcakes. Here are some of the options available, but the key is to use these techniques with your imagination to create fabulous and individual toppers!

FONDANT

This is ideal for rolling flat, cutting out decorations, and molding. When dried hard, the fondant decorations will stand up on the cake and cupcakes to achieve a great three-dimensional effect.

GUM PASTE

This can be used as an alternative to fondant for modeling, as it dries harder. Although edible, it is not palatable. It's ideal for cake toppers, but we would not recommend its use for cupcake decorations.

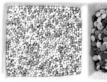

MARZIPAN OR ALMOND PASTE

This can be used as an alternative to fondant and is commonly used to mold fruits and vegetables. It can be a tastier option for larger edible decorations.

PIPING EFFECTS

The frosting recipe on page 13 can be used with a piping bag and tip (or tips) to create many three-dimensional effects, including roses, grass, hair, leaves, and lettering.

CANDIES, NONPAREILS AND SPRINKLES

Ideal for small details such as eyes and noses. Candies can also be rolled out to achieve a new medium.

GLITTERS

Edible glitter adds a sparkle to decorations or frosting.

LUSTER SPRAY

This is used to create a pearlized, gold or silver finish.

EDIBLE INKS AND PAINTS

Edible-ink pens can be used to easily draw or write on hardened fondant. Paint lusters can be mixed with a clear alcohol, like white rum or vodka, and painted onto decorations. The alcohol then evaporates and leaves a painted finish.

OTHER EDIBLES

Cookie crumbs can be used to create sand and dirt effects; chocolate sticks and wafer rolls can be used for structural strength when required.

NON-EDIBLE ALTERNATIVES

Use custom-printed and laminated toppers for a personalized effect. It's easy to craft personalized cupcake toppers using a computer, then print and laminate the results. Laminating ensures that they are food safe, but you should make your guests aware that they are not edible. You can personalize them with names, ages, favorite characters and even photos. The possibilities are endless!

You can also enhance your cakes with store-bought cake toppers. Diamanté initials and brooches provide a classy effect, as do feathers and small bouquets of flowers.

Whether you wish to decorate cupcakes for a school bake sale or create a wedding extravaganza, the designs in the Directory of Cake Toppers will be the center of attention. They are aimed at all levels of experience and are demonstrated step-by-step to make creating fantastic cake toppers easy.

Directory of
cake toppers

BUTTONS
THE BEAR

If you go down to the woods today, you're sure of a big surprise! This cuddly fella is ready for a big hug!

TOOLS AND MATERIALS

Knife or blade tool and rolling pin

Skewer and toothpick or modeling tool

Tan and white fondants

Any metal piping tip

Edible glue and brush

NOTES ON THE CAKE

A 6-inch (15 cm) cake covered in white fondant was used for this design. Handmade tan fondant buttons in two sizes were glued around the base of the cake.

THE BEAR

HOW TO MAKE

STEP 1

★ Roll out a 1¼-inch (3 cm) ball of tan fondant for the body and mold into shape.

★ Roll a 1-inch (2.5 cm) ball for the head and two ¾-inch (2 cm) balls for the arms and legs. Cut the balls for the arms and legs in half to ensure you have an equal amount of fondant for each one.

★ Roll out two ¼-inch (7 mm) balls for the ears.

★ Roll out a ½-inch (1.5 cm) white fondant ball for the snout.

STEP 2

★ Flatten out the white fondant ball for the snout and use the bottom of a metal piping tip to indent the mouth.

★ Roll out the arms and the legs and use the flat end of a skewer to indent the paws on the bottom of the feet.

★ Roll the ears into teardrop shapes and use the end of the skewer or modeling stick to indent the ears, and then pinch the end of the teardrop shape together to make a point.

STEP 3

★ Use the skewer or modeling tool to make two holes in the top of the head and glue the ears into position. Glue the snout onto the head and use a toothpick to mark the eyes. Model a small piece of tan fondant for the nose and glue in place.

★ Sit the body upright and glue the arms and legs in place.

★ Insert a toothpick into the body and secure the head in position; make sure your protruding toothpick is not longer than the head.

★ To make the buttons, take two small white fondant balls, flatten them down with the flat end of the skewer and prick four holes with the toothpick. Glue to the bear's tummy.

BABY CAKES

From baby showers to the new arrival, these adorable cupcakes will have everyone cooing!

TOOLS AND MATERIALS

Knife or blade tool and rolling pin

1¼-inch (3 cm) and 1-inch (2.5 cm) circle cutter for the stroller

¼-inch (7 mm) and ⅓-inch (8 mm) circle cutters

Pale pink fondant

White or pearl nonpareils

Edible glue and brush

THE STROLLER

HOW TO MAKE

STEP 1

★ Roll out the pale pink fondant and cut out a 1¼-inch (3 cm) circle. Using the 1-inch (2.5 cm) circle cutter, indent the larger circle.

★ Roll out two ¼-inch (7 mm) balls of pink fondant and press with your finger to create two ½-inch (1.5 cm) circles for the wheels.

STEP 2

★ Cut out a triangle from the 1¼-inch (3 cm) circle between one and three o'clock. Using a ¼-inch (7 mm) circle cutter, cut out two wheel arches at the base. Roll between your fingers to create a stroller handle.

★ Using the blade tool or knife, indent the hood of the stroller and using the ⅓-inch (8 mm) circle cutter, indent the wheels.

★ Glue the parts together and then glue two white nonpareils into the center of the wheels.

STEP 3

★ Allow to dry for 12 hours and place on a frosted cupcake.

TOOLS AND MATERIALS

Knife or blade tool and rolling pin
....
2¼-inch (5.5 cm) circle cutter
....
Toothpick, skewer and any piping nozzle
....
Marshmallows
....
Skin-colored fondant
....
Pale pink fondant
....
Edible glue and brush

BABES IN BLANKET

HOW TO MAKE

STEP 1

★ For the blanket, roll out the pale pink fondant and cut out a 2¼-inch (5.5 cm) circle. Take a skewer, place it on the edge of the blanket and gently roll up and down to create the frill detail (see page 19).

★ Roll a ball of skin-colored fondant that is ¾-inch (2 cm) in diameter.

STEP 2

★ Mark eyes with a toothpick and indent for the mouth with a piping nozzle. Add a small ball of fondant for the nose.

★ Cut the marshmallow in half lengthwise.

STEP 3

★ Lay the blanket over the half marshmallow, add the baby's head and assemble on the cupcake.

SPOTTY DUCK

This delightful duck is an ideal topper for all things baby: baby showers, new baby, christenings.

TOOLS AND MATERIALS

Knife or blade tool and rolling pin

Pale blue, white, and yellow fondant

No. 5 piping tube or 1/8-inch (3 mm) circle cutter

Toothpick

Edible glue and brush

NOTES ON THE CAKE

A 6 inch (15 cm) cake covered in white fondant, with a coordinating spotty satin ribbon around the base was used here.

THE DUCK

HOW TO MAKE

STEP 1

★ Roll out a 1½-inch (4 cm) ball of pale blue fondant for the body and a 1 inch (2.5 cm) ball for the head.

STEP 2

★ Roll the larger ball at one end and pinch flat to create the tail.

★ Use a toothpick to create the eyes on the head. Make a small triangle of yellow fondant for the beak, and then fix in place with a little edible glue.

★ Glue the head to the body.

STEP 3

★ Cut out the white spots using the piping tube or circle cutter and glue in place.

★ Allow to dry for at least 12 hours.

BABY NAME BLOCKS

These brightly colored play blocks are ideal for a child's christening or first birthday party.

TOOLS AND MATERIALS

Knife or blade tool and rolling pin

7 ounces (200 g) white fondant (makes five blocks)

Tan, yellow, green, blue and red fondants

Small alphabet cutters, less than 1-inch (2.5 cm) square

Selection of small object cutters, less than 1-inch (2.5 cm) square

Edible glue and brush

NOTES ON THE CAKE

A 6-inch (15 cm) round cake covered in tan fondant was used. A red gingham ribbon was tied around the middle with a bow. Secure the bow in place with a pin. Make sure that the pin is removed before serving.

THE NAME BLOCKS

HOW TO MAKE

STEP 1

★ Using a large kitchen knife and white fondant, create a three-dimensional rectangle that is 1-inch (2.5 cm) square and 5-inch (12.5 cm) long. Cut out 1-inch (2.5 cm) cubes for the required number of letter blocks. To make the edges sharper, pinch with your fingers and flatten the sides with a large knife or cake smoother.

STEP 3

★ Glue the letters to the top of the blocks and the objects around the sides.

★ Secure to the top of the cake with either a toothpick or edible glue.

STEP 2

★ Indent each face of the cube with a square border using the blade tool.

★ Roll out the colored fondants to 1/16-inch (1.5 mm) thickness, and cut out your required name with small alphabet cutters in a mixture of fondant colors.

★ Use a selection of small object cutters to decorate your blocks, for example, teddy bear, stars, hearts, butterflies. Or you can cut them out by hand.

NAUTICAL NAME CAKE

Land ahoy! Navigate your little sailor with the aid of this charming nautical-themed cake, ideal for a christening or naming ceremony.

TOOLS AND MATERIALS

Knife or blade tool and rolling pin

Skewer and toothpick

Baby blue, white, red and black fondants

2-inch (5 cm) circle cutter

½-inch (1 cm) and ¼-inch (7 mm) circle cutters

Small star cutter

Star sprinkles

Edible glue and brush

NOTES ON THE CAKE

An 8-inch (20 cm) round cake covered in pale blue fondant was used. A red-striped nautical ribbon was wrapped around the base and secured with a pin at the back, and a life preserver decoration was added to the front. Marble fondant rocks were placed around the base of the lighthouse (see page 17).

Covering cake drums and cake spacers with colored paper and hot-gluing them together created the cake stand, and the edges were trimmed with satin ribbon. This is a great way to create a customized stand.

THE LIGHTHOUSE

HOW TO MAKE

STEP 1

★ Roll a 2-inch (5 cm) ball of white fondant and model into a lighthouse shape, 3 inches (7.5 cm) high.

★ Using red fondant, cut out three strips that measure 4½ x ½ inches (11.5 x 1.5 cm). Glue one at the top of the lighthouse, one at the bottom and one halfway up and cut each strip to length.

STEP 2

★ Cut out a 1½-inch (4 cm) white fondant circle and glue to the top of the lighthouse.

★ Create the light from gray fondant. It should be a cylinder ½ inch (1.5 cm) in diameter by ¾ inch (2 cm) long. Indent a crisscross pattern on it with a blade tool and glue in place. Cut out a ⅛-inch (3 mm) strip of red fondant and glue around the light.

★ Mold a cone to fit on top of the light and indent rings using a circle cutter. Top off with a small rolled ball of fondant.

★ Cut out two windows and a door from black fondant and glue in place.

★ Insert a toothpick into the base of the lighthouse and leave to dry for 24 hours.

THE BOAT

HOW TO MAKE

STEP 1

★ Roll and cut out a 1½-inch (4 cm) high white fondant triangle for the sail, then roll out and cut out a baby blue triangle sail. Glue the sails to a toothpick.

★ Roll and cut out two red fondant stripes and glue to the blue sail. Glue a red star sprinkle to the white sail.

★ Roll and cut out a three-dimensional hull shape that is 1 inch (2.5 cm) long from the red fondant.

STEP 2

★ Cut out a small red circle and a small white circle. Cut the red circle into eight parts and glue four of the parts onto the white circle to create a life buoy.

THE NAUTICAL FLAG CUPCAKE

HOW TO MAKE

★ Flat-fondant a cupcake with baby blue fondant as shown on page 17.

★ Roll out some white fondant and cut out a triangle to fit on your cupcake.

★ Roll out some red fondant and cut out the required letter and a strip for the bunting ribbon.

★ Glue the triangle, letter and ribbon to the frosted cupcake and use the end of a sharp knife to indent a stitching pattern.

THE BOAT CUPCAKE TOPPER

HOW TO MAKE

★ Roll out and cut a white fondant triangle sail that is 1½ inches (4 cm) high, then roll out and cut out a baby blue triangle sail.

★ Roll out the red fondant and cut out a flat hull shape that is 1 inch (2.5 cm) long.

★ Roll out and cut two red fondant stripes and glue to the blue sail. Glue a red star sprinkle to the white sail.

THE LIGHTHOUSE
CUPCAKE TOPPER

HOW TO MAKE

★ Cut out a lighthouse shape from white fondant that is
1 inch (2.5 cm) high.

★ Cut a triangle roof from red fondant.

★ Cut three red strips and glue into position.

★ Cut a door and window from black fondant and
glue in place.

THE ANCHOR
CUPCAKE TOPPER

HOW TO MAKE

★ Roll a baby blue sausage shape for the main shank.

★ Mold an arc for the base and glue to the shank.

★ Cut a small ball in half, roll each one and glue to the
main shank.

★ Roll a thin sausage, curl it round to make the top ring
and glue in place.

Tiptoe into an enchanted land where these magical creatures dwell!

TOOLS AND MATERIALS

Knife or blade tool and rolling pin

Pale blue, pale yellow, pale pink, red and white fondants

Toothpick and any metal piping tip

Small flower cutter

Edible glitter

Edible glue and brush

CORY THE CATERPILLAR

HOW TO MAKE

STEP 1

★ Roll four ½-inch (1.5 cm) balls of pale blue fondant.

★ Roll an ⅛-inch (3 mm) ball of blue fondant and cut in half.

★ To create the mushroom, roll out a ½-inch (1.5 cm) ball of red fondant and a ball of white fondant.

STEP 2

★ Glue the four blue balls together to create the caterpillar, mark his eyes with a toothpick and make an indent for his mouth with a piping tip.

★ To make the feelers, roll the small blue halves of fondant into thin sausages.

★ To create the top of the mushroom, use a ball tool to press the red fondant ball into the palm of your hand. Roll the white fondant into a cone shape to create the mushroom stalk.

STEP 3

★ Use a toothpick to create a hole in the caterpillar's head for the feelers and glue them in.

★ Roll small balls of white fondant and glue them to the top of the mushroom. Glue the top of the mushroom to the stalk.

SALLY THE SNAIL

HOW TO MAKE

STEP 1

★ Roll the yellow fondant into a sausage about 6 inches (15 cm) long and ¼ inch (7 mm) thick. Smooth half of the sausage flat with your finger and, starting from the thinner end, curl it around itself to create the shell.

★ Create the head and body from pink fondant and prick two eyes and an indent for the mouth with a piping tip.

★ For the feelers, roll two small pink sausages and indent halfway with a skewer.

STEP 2

★ Glue the shell to the body and trim any excess with a knife.

★ Make a hole with a toothpick for the feelers and glue in place.

★ Use a small flower cutter to create flowers in pink fondant, and attach a small ball of yellow fondant to the centers with glue.

STEP 3

★ Frost the cupcake with grass using green buttercream and a grass tip (see page 15).

★ Assemble the creatures, mushrooms and flowers and sprinkle with magic dust (edible glitter)!

VERITY THE FAIRY

Verity is a special little fairy who lives in an enchanted garden. If you are lucky, she may grant you a wish!

TOOLS AND MATERIALS

Knife or blade tool and rolling pin

Toothpicks and skewer or no.3 modeling tool

Purple, pink, skin color, yellow, white and green fondants

Butterfly and ¼-inch (7 mm) flower cutter

Any metal piping tube

Edible glue and brush

NOTES ON THE CAKE

A 6-inch (15 cm) cake, covered in green fondant was used for this design. Green frosting was piped around the base using the grass technique (see page 15) and some flowers were also added. The grass frosting was also used to affix Verity and the mushrooms to the top of the cake.

VERITY

HOW TO MAKE

STEP 1

★ Roll out a 1-inch (2.5 cm) ball of skin-colored fondant for the body and mold into shape. Allow to dry for an hour.

★ Roll a ¾-inch (2 cm) ball for the head and two ½-inch (1 cm) balls for the arms and legs. Cut each of these in half to ensure you have an equal amount of fondant for each one. Mold into shape.

★ Roll out the purple fondant and cut out a 3-inch (7.5 cm) diameter circle.

★ Roll out the pink fondant and cut out the butterfly wings.

STEP 3

★ To make the top of the mushroom, use a ball tool to press a pink fondant ball into the palm of your hand. Roll some white fondant into a cone shape to create the mushroom stalk.

★ Roll small balls of white fondant and glue to the top of the mushroom. Glue the top of the mushroom to the stalk.

★ Cut out three green fondant leaves. Place toothpicks on the bottom quarter of the leaves, gently pinch the fondant over the toothpick, and leave to dry for 24 hours.

★ When the fairy and leaves are dry, assemble on the cake.

STEP 2

★ Sit the body upright and glue the legs into position.

★ Place the purple fondant circle over the body and smooth down to make the dress.

★ Glue the arms into position and fix the butterfly wings to Verity's back.

★ Insert a toothpick into the fairy and place the head onto the toothpick.

★ Use a toothpick to mark the eyes and a piping tube to indent the mouth; roll a small piece of fondant for the nose and glue in place.

★ Roll out long, thin sausage shapes from yellow fondant and glue to the fairy's head as hair.

★ Cut out small flowers and glue to the hair.

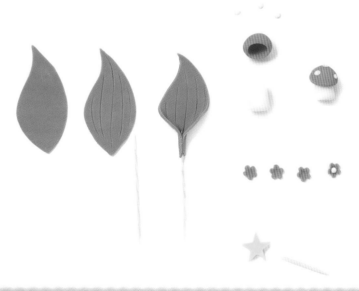

DIGGER, TRACTOR AND FIRE ENGINE

Vroom! Take a ride with every boy's favorite vehicles to do some digging, plowing or putting out fires!

TOOLS AND MATERIALS

Knife or blade tool and a rolling pin

Yellow, gray, black, green and red fondants

1-inch (2.5 cm) circle cutter

Edible glue and brush

Black edible-ink pen

THE DIGGER

HOW TO MAKE

STEP 1

★ Cut out a 2-inch (5 cm) by ¼-inch (7 mm) rectangle of yellow fondant and create an indent at the top.

★ Cut out a 1-inch (2.5 cm) circle from the yellow fondant, and cut again to create a crescent for the digger bucket. Cut a small 1-inch (2.5 cm) by ¼-inch (7 mm) strip to create the roof and two 1-inch (2.5 cm) by ⅛-inch (3 mm) strips to make fenders.

STEP 2

★ Cut a 1-inch (2.5 cm) square of gray fondant for the cab and a small square for the engine (indent with the knife).

★ Roll two ½-inch (1 cm) black fondant balls and two ¼-inch (7 mm) yellow fondant balls. Press each of the yellow fondant balls into the black balls to create two wheels. Attach the yellow fenders to the top of the wheels.

STEP 3

★ Glue all the parts together. Attach the bucket and digger with a strip of yellow fondant.

★ Allow to dry. Place carefully on top of a whip-frosted cupcake.

THE TRACTOR

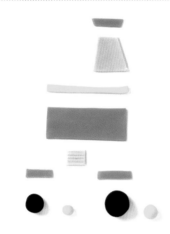

HOW TO MAKE

STEP 1

★ Cut a green fondant rectangle that is 2 inches (5 cm) by 1 inch (2.5 cm) to create the tractor base. Cut another for the roof that is 1 inch (2.5 cm) by ¼ inch (7 mm) and two 1-inch (2.5 cm) by ⅛-inch (3 mm) strips for the fenders.

★ Cut a 1-inch (2.5 cm) square from gray fondant to create the window. Cut a small rectangle and indent with a knife to create the engine.

THE FIRE ENGINE

HOW TO MAKE

STEP 1

★ Cut a 2-inch (5 cm) by 1¼-inch (3 cm) rectangle of red fondant and cut out an indent to create a cab shape at the front.

★ Roll three ¼-inch (7 mm) black balls to create wheels with ⅛-inch (3 mm) gray fondant wheel inserts.

STEP 2

★ As you did for the digger, create the wheels with one ¾-inch (2 cm) black ball and one ½-inch (1.5 cm) black ball. Insert with ¼-inch (7 mm) yellow balls.

★ Glue the fenders to the tops of the wheels.

STEP 3

★ Glue all of the parts together.

★ Allow to dry. Place carefully on top of a whip-frosted cupcake.

STEP 2

★ Cut out a small black rectangle for the cab window.

★ Cut one small square and a small rectangle in gray fondant and indent with a knife to create engines and drawers.

★ Cut a 1¼-inch (3 cm) yellow strip and indent to create the ladder.

STEP 3

★ Glue the parts together.

★ Allow to dry before placing on top of a frosted cupcake.

BOBO THE CLOWN

Roll up! Roll up! It will be smiles all around with this lovable clown.

TOOLS AND MATERIALS

Knife or blade tool and rolling pin

Skewer and toothpick or no.3 modeling tool

Blue, green, white, red, orange and yellow fondants

Edible glue and brush

Any metal piping tip

Sugar-craft wire

¼-inch (7 mm) flower cutter

1¼-inch (3 cm) circle cutter

NOTES ON THE CAKE

A 6-inch (15 cm) round cake covered in white fondant was used. A rainbow ribbon was placed around the base and secured at the back with a pin. Always remove any pins before serving.

BOBO

HOW TO MAKE

STEP 1

★ In blue fondant, roll a 1-inch (2.5 cm) ball for the body and two ½-inch (1.5 cm) balls for the arms and legs. Cut each of these in half to ensure you have an equal amount of fondant for each one. Roll a thin sausage for the hat trim.

★ Roll a ¾-inch (2 cm) green fondant ball for the hat.

★ Roll a 1-inch (2.5 cm) white fondant ball for the head.

★ Roll two ¼-inch (7 mm) orange fondant balls for the hair.

★ Roll out a ½-inch (1.5 cm) red fondant ball for the feet and cut in half. Roll four ¼-inch (7 mm) red fondant balls for the pom-poms and nose.

★ Roll out and cut a 1¼-inch (3 cm) green fondant circle for the ruffle.

STEP 3

★ Glue the hat to the head, attach the hat trim and glue the hair in place.

★ Glue the arms to the body and insert a cocktail stick halfway into the body. You can now use this to hold your clown while you glue the ruffle and head into position.

★ Glue on the nose and pom-poms.

★ Roll out and cut out a small flower from yellow fondant. Add a small red ball to the center of the flower and glue to Bobo's hat.

★ To make the balloon, roll a yellow fondant ball and flatten it with your finger. Bend the wire and insert gently into the balloon. Leave to dry.

★ Use a piece of the wire to make a hole through the body (which will later hold the balloon and wire). Keep it close to the arm to prevent the wire from falling back.

★ When everything has dried, insert the toothpick in the clown's body between the feet and into the cake so that the stick and the legs support the body.

★ Insert the balloon wire through the hole in the body and place on top of the cake.

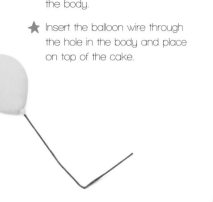

STEP 2

★ Roll the body into shape and the arms into sausage shapes. Lay the half balls for the legs on their flat-cut sides and twist to create the legs.

★ For the feet, roll the two halves into teardrop shapes, flatten out the pointed ends with your finger and cut the point away with the round cutter.

★ Take a skewer and make the ruffle using the frilling technique shown on page 19.

★ Use a toothpick to mark the eyes in the head and the metal piping tip base to indent for the mouth.

★ Roll the green fondant ball into a cone for the hat.

★ Roll the orange fondant balls into sausages and use a blade tool to mark the hair.

FARM

Create this fabulous farm cake in two shakes of a lamb's tail!

TOOLS AND MATERIALS

Knife or craft knife and rolling pin

White, pink, black, yellow, red, brown and orange fondants

1¾-inch (4.5 cm) circle cutter

1¾-inch (4.5 cm) scalloped circle cutter

¼-inch (7 mm) and ⅛-inch (3 mm) flower cutters

Skewer or toothpick

Edible glue and brush

NOTES ON THE CAKE

An 8-inch (20 cm) round cake covered in pastel green fondant was used. The fence was created using wood effect fondant (see page 17). Some animal cupcake toppers were added to the sides of the cake.

The base was piped with green frosting using a grass effect (see page 14). Marble fondant stones and flowers were added for decoration.

Shredded wheat was used to make the hay bales, and the pond was modeled using water effect fondant (see page 17). Green frosting with a grass effect was piped around the edge.

THE PIG

HOW TO MAKE

★ Roll out the pink fondant to ⅛ inch (3 mm) thick and cut out a 1¾-inch (4.5 cm) diameter circle.

★ Also in pink fondant roll out a ¼-inch (7 mm) ball for the snout and an ⅛-inch (3 mm) ball, which will form the ears.

★ Press the snout ball with your finger and use a skewer to mark the nose and a metal piping tip to mark the mouth.

★ Cut the ear fondant into two and roll into balls. Flatten with your finger and pinch each end to create an ear. Repeat with the other half.

★ Glue the parts together, add two small black fondant balls as eyes and thinly rolled pink fondant for the hair.

THE HORSE

HOW TO MAKE

★ Roll out the brown fondant to ⅛ inch (3 mm) thick, cut out a ¼-inch (7 mm) diameter circle for the snout and mark the nose and mouth as for the pig.

★ Roll out two ¼-inch (7 mm) balls of brown fondant and two ⅛-inch (3 mm) balls of pink fondant. Flatten the pink fondant ball on top of the brown fondant ball with your finger and pinch each end to create an ear. Repeat with the other half.

★ Cut out a small triangle of tan fondant and cut triangles from the base to create the mane. Cut a thin triangle from white fondant to match the face markings.

★ Glue all of the parts together and add two small black fondant balls for eyes.

>

THE DUCK

HOW TO MAKE

★ Roll out the yellow fondant and cut out a 1¾-inch (4.5 cm) circle. Roll out a small amount of orange fondant and cut out a beak shape—do this by using the 1¾-inch circle cutter to cut a wedge from the orange fondant circle. You should be left with a triangle with curving edges. Roll two thin sausages of yellow fondant for the hair.

★ Glue all the parts together and add two small black fondant balls for the eyes.

THE CHICKEN

HOW TO MAKE

★ Roll out the white and red fondant to ⅛ inch (3 mm) thick. Cut out a 1¾-inch (4.5 cm) circle from the white and, using the 1¾-inch (4.5 cm) scalloped cutter as the edge, cut out a comb and wattle from the red fondant.

★ Roll out a small piece of yellow fondant and cut out two small diamond shapes, one bigger than the other, for the beak. Glue all of the parts together and add two small black fondant balls for the eyes.

THE COW

HOW TO MAKE

★ Roll out the white fondant to ⅛ inch (3 mm) thick and cut out a 1¾-inch (4.5 cm) circle.

★ In pink fondant, roll a ½-inch (1 cm) ball for the snout and mark two nostrils with a skewer. Cut out a tiny ⅛-inch (3 mm) flower in yellow fondant and attach as the mouth. Create the ears using white and pink fondant balls.

★ Roll out the black fondant and cut out a ¼-inch (7 mm) flower as the hair. Using the 1¾-inch (4.5 cm) scalloped circle cutter, cut out the various face markings.

★ Glue all the parts together and add two small black fondant balls as eyes.

THE SHEEP

HOW TO MAKE

★ Roll out the white fondant to ⅛ inch (3 mm) thick and, using a 1¾ inch (4.5 cm) scalloped circle cutter, cut out the face. Also cut out a ½ inch (1 cm) flower for the hair. Roll out a small amount of pink fondant, cut out a ½ inch (1 cm) flower for the nose, and mark the nostrils with a skewer.

★ Roll out a ½ inch (1 cm) ball of white fondant and a ⅛ inch (3 mm) ball of black fondant. Flatten the black into the white ball with your finger. Cut the circle in half and pinch the flat edge together to create an ear. Repeat with the other half.

★ Glue all the parts together and add two small black fondant balls as eyes.

THE CHICKEN

HOW TO MAKE

★ Roll a ¾-inch (2 cm) ball of white fondant for the body and a ½-inch (1 cm) ball for the head. Mold the body with a tail and cut two triangles out of the tail to create feathers.

★ Using yellow fondant, mold a small triangular beak and glue to the head. Create two eyes using a toothpick.

★ Roll out two small red fondant balls, mold a wattle and comb and glue to the head. Glue the head to the body and place on a nest made of shredded wheat.

THE DUCK

HOW TO MAKE

★ Roll out two small ¼-inch (7 mm) and ½-inch (1.5 cm) balls of yellow fondant. Mold the larger ball as the duck's body along with the tail. Glue the head in place and add two eyes with a toothpick. Mold a small beak from orange fondant and glue in place.

★ Roll out a ¼-inch (7 mm) ball of yellow fondant and press with your finger. Cut in half and glue to the side of the duck's body as wings.

>

THE BARN

HOW TO MAKE

★ Mix some brown and red fondants to create a rust color and roll out to ¼ inch (7 mm) thick. Cut out a rectangle that is 4 x 3 inches (10 x 7.5 cm). Cut the top quarter portion to create the Dutch roof effect as shown. Use the knife and toothpick to create a wood-paneled effect.

★ Roll out some white fondant to ¼ inch (7 mm) thick, cut out ¼-inch (7 mm) strips, and glue to the side of the barn, allowing the roof to overlap to create eaves. Roll out the black fondant, cut a ¼-inch (7 mm) wide strip and glue to form the roof.

★ To create the barn door, roll out the white fondant to ⅛ inch (3 mm) thick and cut a ¼-inch (7 mm) wide strip. Use this strip to create a square box with a cross inside, and glue to the front of the barn.

★ To create the window, roll out the black fondant and cut out a rectangle that is 1 x 1½ inches (2.5 x 4 cm) and trim with thin strips of white fondant. Glue in place.

THE WEATHER VANE

HOW TO MAKE

★ Using black fondant, roll a ¼-inch (7 mm) ball for the head and a ½-inch (1 cm) ball for the body. Mold the body with a tail and cut two triangles out of the tail to create feathers.

★ Mold a small beak and comb, glue to the rooster's head and then glue the head to the body.

★ Roll one small sausage from black fondant and insert the toothpick through it. Cut two ¾ inch (2 cm) wide strips to form the cross at the base of the weather vane. Insert the toothpick through the center of the cross and attach it to the base of the rooster.

★ Assemble the weather vane on a skewer. First add one of the small balls, then add the cross, the other small ball, and then the rooster. Insert into some spare fondant and allow to dry for 24 hours. Insert into the top of the barn before assembling on the cake.

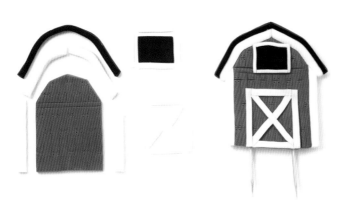

PIRATE TREASURE ISLAND

Come aboard with these swashbuckling pirates and bag yourself some treasure!

COOL CAKE TOPPERS

TOOLS AND MATERIALS

Knife or craft knife and rolling pin

Black, white, yellow and red fondants

Wood effect fondant (see page 17)

1⅓-inch (3.5 cm) and 3-inch (7.5 cm) circle cutters

Black edible ink pen

Edible gold paint and brush

Clear alcohol (white rum or vodka)

Round yellow sprinkles

White ball sprinkles

Gold foil chocolate coins

NOTES ON THE CAKE

An 8-inch (20 cm) round cake covered with parchment-effect fondant (see page 17) was used here. The fondant on the cake was left to dry for 24 hours, and then a compass and treasure map details were drawn on the cake in black edible ink. The chest is placed on a pile of graham cracker crumbs and the base is surrounded with black fondant cannonballs.

THE TREASURE CHEST

HOW TO MAKE

STEP 1

★ Using the wood-effect fondant, cut three rectangles that are 1 x 2½ inches (2.5 x 6.5 cm), for the base, front and back of the chest.

★ Cut out one rectangle that is 1½ x 2½ inches (4 cm x 6.5 cm), for the lid and two 1-inch (2.5 cm) squares for the chest ends.

★ Cut a 1⅓-inch (3.5 cm) diameter circle and cut it in two for the lid ends.

★ Lay the largest rectangle (the lid) over a rolling pin and allow to set overnight.

★ After the other parts have dried for 15 minutes, glue the box together and allow to dry overnight.

STEP 2

★ Roll out the yellow fondant, cut out ¼-inch (7 mm) strips and glue to the edges of the treasure chest. Glue on round yellow sprinkles as the rivets.

★ Paint the yellow edging with gold edible paint.

STEP 3

★ Using yellow fondant, mold a keyhole and two handles for each end of the chest. Dot the keyhole with black edible ink and glue to the chest.

★ When dry, fill the chest with gold chocolate coins and a pearl necklace made out of a thin sausage of white fondant with white ball sprinkles glued on. The chest is ready to place on top of your cake.

THE GOLD BOOTY

HOW TO MAKE

★ Simply add gold foil chocolate coins to frosted cupcakes and sprinkles with edible gold glitter.

THE SKULL AND CROSSBONES

HOW TO MAKE

STEP 1

★ Roll out the black fondant and cut out a 3-inch (7.5 cm) diameter circle.

★ Roll out the white fondant and cut out the pirate skull using the template on page 141. Using a skewer, poke out the skull's eyes and nose. Use the knife to indent the teeth

STEP 2

★ From the rolled white fondant, cut four ¼ x ¾ inch (7 mm x 2 cm) strips. Cut the tip of one end of a fondant strip and press with your finger to form the bones. Repeat this with all of the strips.

STEP 3

★ Glue the skull to the black disk and glue the four bones around the skull, trimming any excess bone.

★ Allow to dry for 24 hours and place on a flat-frosted cupcake.

CUTE CUPCAKE TOPPERS

Cute! Cute! Cute!
Adorable little additions to a girl's best friend...cupcakes!

TOOLS AND MATERIALS

Knife or blade tool and rolling pin

Pastel yellow, white and black fondants

Pink jellybean

Edible glue and brush

Plastic wrap

THE HAMSTER

HOW TO MAKE

STEP 1

★ Roll 1¼-inch (3 cm) and ⅛-inch (3 mm) balls of pastel yellow fondant. Also roll a ¼-inch (7 mm) ball of white fondant and flatten it with your finger to create the face.

★ Mold the hamster's body by placing your finger on the ball and rolling it back and forth.

STEP 2

★ Cut the small ball of yellow fondant in half and roll into two balls. Place each ball under some plastic wrap and press one side flat with your finger. Remove the wrap and curl the thin side to create an ear; repeat with the other half.

★ Roll two small eyes from black fondant and cut the jellybean in half to create the nose.

STEP 3

★ Glue the face, eyes, nose and ears to the hamster. Indent the body with a blade tool to create fore and hind legs.

★ Allow to dry and place on a frosted cupcake.

TOOLS AND MATERIALS

Knife or blade tool and rolling pin

1¾-inch (4.5 cm) circle cutter

Pastel pink and pastel yellow fondants

Flower shaper tool

Toothpick and skewer

Any metal piping tip

Edible glue and brush

THE PONY

HOW TO MAKE

STEP 1

★ Roll out a small amount of white fondant and cut out a 1¾-inch (4.5 cm) diameter circle.

★ Roll out a 1-inch (2.5 cm) ball of pastel yellow fondant and mold into a pony's head shape.

★ Roll out a small amount of pastel yellow fondant and cut out two small triangles for the ears.

STEP 2

★ Mark eyes with a toothpick and indent for the mouth with a piping tip. Add two nostrils with a skewer.

★ Using the flower shaper tool, indent the pony's ears and glue to the head.

STEP 3

★ Cut out the pony's mane and face markings, as shown, from the circle. Attach to the pony's head. Using a knife, indent the pony's mane to create the hair effect.

★ Allow to dry and place on a frosted cupcake.

TOOLS AND MATERIALS

Knife or blade tool and a rolling pin

Pale pink fondant

Pale pink buttercream

Wilton no.104 petal tip

Edible glitter

Template for the ballerina's bodice (see page 140)

THE BALLERINA

HOW TO MAKE

STEP 1

★ Use the template (see page 140) to cut out the ballerina's bodice from pale pink fondant.

STEP 2

★ Use a Wilton no.104 petal tip to pipe frills for the ballerina's skirt on the cake. Starting from the center, work to the edge and back and complete a ring of piped loops.

★ Repeat twice more to create the full skirt.

STEP 3

★ Place the ballerina's bodice into the piped skirt and sprinkle with edible glitter.

CUTE CUPCAKE CHARACTERS

These cute little cupcake toppers will soon become any girl's new best friend!

TOOLS AND MATERIALS

A selection of pink, yellow, lilac, hot pink and black fondants

Knife or blade tool and a rolling pin

Paintbrush and edible glue

BLUSH

HOW TO MAKE

STEP 1

★ Roll out a 1½-inch (4 cm) ball of pink fondant and roll into a tear shape.

★ Make a cut in the top to make the heart shape.

★ Use your fingers to smooth out the heart shape and any rough edges.

STEP 2

★ To make the bow, roll out the hot pink fondant, cut out two small triangles and glue them together. Add a small ball to the center and indent the bow using the blade tool or the back of a knife.

STEP 3

★ Take two small balls of black fondant to create the eyes and roll out slightly with your finger to elongate.

★ Glue the bow and eyes to the heart.

★ Allow to dry for at least 12 hours.

TWINKLE

HOW TO MAKE

STEP 1

★ Roll out a ball of yellow fondant to ½ inch (1.5 cm) thick and mark out and cut out a star shape.

★ Use your fingers to smooth out the star shape and any rough edges.

STEP 2

★ To make the bow, roll out the hot pink fondant, cut out two small triangles and glue them together. Add a small ball to the center and indent for the bow using the blade tool or the back of a knife.

STEP 3

★ Take two small balls of black fondant for the eyes and roll out slightly with your finger to elongate.

★ Glue the bow and eyes to the star.

★ Allow to dry for at least 12 hours.

DEWDROP

HOW TO MAKE

STEP 1

★ Roll out a 1½-inch (4 cm) ball of lilac fondant and roll into a teardrop shape.

★ Use your fingers to smooth out the shape and any rough edges. Pinch the top of the teardrop shape and bend into place.

STEP 2

★ To make the bow, roll out the hot pink fondant, cut out two small triangles and glue them together. Add a small ball to the center and indent for the bow using the blade tool or the back of a knife.

STEP 3

★ Take two small balls of black fondant for the eyes and roll out slightly with your finger to elongate.

★ Glue the bow and eyes to the drop.

★ Allow to dry for at least 12 hours.

DARCY, DOG IN A HANDBAG

Darcy is a fluffy little friend you can carry with you anywhere!

TOOLS AND MATERIALS

Knife and rolling pin

Pale pink, hot pink and black fondants

Toothpicks

¼-inch (7 mm) circle cutter

1-inch (2.5 cm) circle cutter

Ball tool and flower tool

Small pearl ball sprinkles

Edible glue and brush

NOTES ON THE CAKE

A 6-inch (15 cm) round cake covered in pale pink fondant was used. A black ribbon was placed around the base and secured with a pin at the back. Cut out paw prints made from black fondant have been glued to the side of the cake while still pliable.

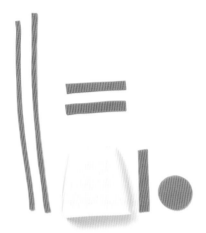

THE HANDBAG

HOW TO MAKE

STEP 1

★ Mold a handbag shape from pale pink fondant that is 2 inches (5 cm) at the base and tapers to 1½-inches (4 cm) at the top.

★ Roll out some hot pink fondant to ⅛ inch (3 mm) thick and cut out two 1-inch (2.5 cm) diameter circles for the pockets. Also cut out three 2-inch (5 cm) strips for the handles and the vertical detail. You will also need to cut out two 6 x ¼-inch (15 cm x 7 mm) strips for the bag's trim.

STEP 2

★ Glue the trim and handles onto the handbag.

★ Cut across the circles, three-quarters of the way up, and indent creases in the larger bottom section using the knife. Invert the top section and glue to the base to create the lid of the pockets. Glue on a small pearl sprinkle as the button.

★ Cut a 2 x ¼-inch (5 cm x 7 mm) strip of hot pink fondant and glue both ends at the center to create a bow. Add a small rectangle to the center of the bow and glue to the front of the bag.

★ Mold a small heart from hot pink fondant and attach to the bag with a thin sausage of hot pink to create a tag.

DARCY

HOW TO MAKE

★ Roll out a 1-inch (2.5 cm) ball of white fondant and then mold it into the shape of the dog's head, including a snout and ears.

★ Using a bone tool, indent for the eyes. Indent for the ears using a flower tool. Using a ¼-inch (7 mm) round cutter, indent the lips twice, and use the flower tool to create a mouth. Add two small white fondant eyebrows.

★ Glue two black fondant balls in place as eyes and a black fondant triangular nose, pricked twice with a toothpick.

★ Using the tip of the knife, fluff the face to create hair all over the head. Use a small piece of hot pink fondant to create a tongue and indent with a vertical line. Glue the tongue into the mouth. Create a bow from hot pink fondant with two small triangles and a tiny ball for the center. Glue on top of the dog's head.

★ Insert a toothpick into the base of the head and then place into the top of the handbag.

★ Leave to dry for 24 hours and place on top of the cake.

PRINCESS

Play fairy godmother and make your little princess's dreams come true with this enchanting cake topper.

TOOLS AND MATERIALS

Mini doll pick

Knife or blade tool

Rolling pin

Toothpick and skewer or modeling tool

Small heart cutter

Muffin-sized cupcake and mini-cupcake

Heart sprinkles

Pearl nonpareils

NOTES ON THE CAKE

A 6-inch (15 cm) round cake covered in pale pink fondant was used, with a hot pink polka-dot ribbon around the base secured at the back with a pin. Make sure to remove the pin before serving.

THE PRINCESS

HOW TO MAKE

STEP 1

★ Use a toothpick to fix a mini cupcake to an upturned cupcake and insert the doll so that the cupcakes form the base of the skirt.

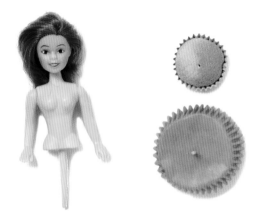

STEP 2

★ Roll out the pink fondant and cut out the bodice shape to fit the doll; glue in place on the doll.

★ Roll out the white fondant and cut out the underskirt and frill strips.

★ Use the technique shown on page 19 to frill the skirt strips.

★ Drape the underskirt over the center of the doll and glue the frills in place.

STEP 3

★ Roll out the pink fondant, cut out a kidney shape for the skirt and place it around the doll. Glue in place.

★ Use the pearls to decorate the underskirt and neaten the join between the skirt and bodice. Glue heart sprinkles in place.

★ Roll out the pink fondant and cut out a crown shape. This can be done easily by using a small heart cutter.

★ Glue some pearls to the points of the crown and a heart sprinkle to the front and fix the crown in place.

★ Leave to dry for 24 hours.

These are some rootin' tootin' Wild West cupcakes! And for the foosball fan, there's an awesome foosball player!

TOOLS AND MATERIALS

Knife or blade tool and rolling pin

Red fondant

White candy stick

Edible glue and brush

THE FOOSBALL PLAYER

HOW TO MAKE

STEP 1

★ Roll a red fondant sausage that is 1 inch (2.5 cm) x ½ inch (1.5 cm), another sausage that is ¾ inch (2 cm) x ½ inch (1.5 cm) and a ½-inch (1.5 cm) ball for the head.

STEP 2

★ Mold the larger sausage to create the body. Use the blade tool to indent the legs and shorts.

★ Mold the smaller sausage between your fingers to create a base with sharp edges.

STEP 3

★ Gently push the candy stick through the upper body.

★ Glue the base and head onto the body and allow to dry for 24 hours.

★ Place on a frosted cupcake.

TOOLS AND MATERIALS

Knife or blade tool and rolling pin

Brown, black, yellow, blue and red fondants

2¼-inch (5.5 cm) circle cutter

½-inch (1.5 cm) star cutter

A marshmallow cutter

Edible glue and brush

THE FEATHER HEADDRESS

HOW TO MAKE

STEP 1

★ Roll black fondant into three 8-inch (20 cm) long, thin sausages and braid them by folding one over the next. Apply the braid around the edge of a black flat fondant-covered cupcake with glue.

STEP 2

★ Roll out the yellow fondant and cut out a 2¼-inch (6 cm) diameter circle with a cutter; use the same cutter to cut out a feather shape.

★ Pinch the end of the feather and cut the feather edges with the knife. Repeat with red and blue fondants to create more feathers.

STEP 3

★ When dry, cut a small hole in the back of the cupcake and add glue. Carefully insert a feather so that it is upright. Repeat with the other feathers.

THE COWBOY HAT

HOW TO MAKE

STEP 1

★ Roll out the brown fondant and cut out a 3-inch (7.5 cm) diameter circle for the base, lay it flat on some parchment paper and prop up two edges with pencils.

★ Roll out brown fondant and cut out a 2¼-inch (6 cm) diameter circle and place it over a marshmallow with a "V" shape cut into it. Mold the fondant over the marshmallow and trim the edge to create the top of the hat.

STEP 2

★ Roll out a small amount of yellow fondant and use a ½-inch (1.27 cm) star-shaped cutter to create a sheriff's badge. Glue small yellow fondant balls to each point of the star.

STEP 3

★ Glue the top and bottom of the hat together, glue the sheriff's badge to front of the hat and place on a frosted cupcake.

ARMY

*I don't know but I've been told,
for army cupcakes you're never too old!*

TOOLS AND MATERIALS

Knife or blade tool and a rolling pin

Green, brown, black, tan and gray fondants

2¾-inch (7 cm) circle cutter

Edible silver paint

Edible silver luster spray

White nonpareils

Mini alphabet craft stamps

Templates for the badge and dog tags (see page 140)

CAMOUFLAGE

HOW TO MAKE

STEP 1

★ Pinch small amounts of the black, brown and tan fondant and roll between your fingers. Then roll flat with a rolling pin.

STEP 2

★ Roll out green fondant and scatter the pieces on top. Cover with plastic wrap and roll flat with a rolling pin.

STEP 3

★ Cut out a 2¾-inch (7 cm) circle from the camouflage fondant and flat-frost onto a cupcake (see page 17).

THE DOG TAGS

HOW TO MAKE

STEP 1

★ Using gray fondant, cut out two dog tag shapes using the template (see page 140) and create a thin gray sausage for the chain.

STEP 2

★ Using the alphabet craft stamps, indent your message or a name on one of the dog tags.

THE ARMY BADGE

HOW TO MAKE

STEP 1

★ Roll out green fondant and cut a badge shape using the template (see page 140).

STEP 2

★ Cut out three gray "V" shapes using a knife and glue to the badge.

STEP 3

★ Glue the badge to a black flat fondant-covered cupcake. When dry, paint the gray stripes with edible silver paint.

STEP 3

★ Assemble the dog tags and chain. Glue the nonpareils in place to create the chain effect. Apply the edible silver luster spray and, when dry, place on top of a green flat fondant-covered cupcake.

These freaky little fellas will provide a peculiar twist to any bash!

TOOLS AND MATERIALS

Knife or blade tool and a rolling pin

Red, black, yellow, blue, orange, white and purple fondants

Small paintbrush with either a little water or edible glue

Black edible ink pen

Two small purple candies

ROYSTON THE MONSTER

HOW TO MAKE

STEP 1

★ Roll out some red fondant to ½ inch (1.5 cm) thick and cut into a rectangular shape to create the body. Use your fingers to smooth out the shape and any rough edges.

★ Use the blade tool to mark the legs.

STEP 2

★ Roll a sausage shape in red fondant to create the arms and cut to the right length.

★ Roll out some yellow fondant and cut a small rectangle for the mouth. Roll out a strip of blue fondant and cut out triangles for the teeth.

STEP 3

★ Assemble all the parts and glue together adding two small black fondant balls for eyes.

★ Allow to dry for at least 12 hours.

SHARK BITE

HOW TO MAKE

STEP 1

★ Mold a fat sausage shape from orange fondant, tapering it at one end. Use your finger to roll the tapered end and create an indent. Give the shark a pointed nose.

STEP 2

★ Mold two fins from black fondant and attach to the shark with edible glue.

★ Using a knife, cut the base to create two feet.

STEP 3

* To create the mouth, cut a black fondant triangle, a smaller white fondant triangle and black triangle teeth. Affix the layers with edible glue and attach to the shark.

* Roll a small black fondant ball to create an eye.

* Allow to dry for at least 12 hours.

LIGHTNING MAN

HOW TO MAKE

STEP 1

* Mold a head from a 1-inch (2.5 cm) purple fondant ball and mold the body from a ½-inch (1.5 cm) purple fondant ball.

* Create a white belly by rolling a small white fondant ball and pushing it into a flat, oblong shape. Glue to the body.

STEP 2

* Roll a small ball of purple fondant into a sausage shape and cut in two to create arms. Glue between the head and body.

* Glue two purple candies to the belly, as feet.

STEP 3

* Roll out a small piece of black fondant and, with a knife, cut out a lightning shape for his antenna and a cross for his eye. Glue in place.

* Roll out a small and larger ball of white fondant to create the other eye and the nose, and attach with glue.

* Allow to dry for at least 12 hours.

COOL DUDES

If you want to rock, skate, or just hang out with the cool dudes, then these cupcakes are just for you!

TOOLS AND MATERIALS

Knife or craft knife and rolling pin

White and black fondants

Selection of edible-ink pens, including black

Skewer

Edible glue and brush

THE SKATEBOARD

HOW TO MAKE

STEP 1

★ Roll out the white fondant to a ⅛-inch (3 mm) thickness and cut out the skateboard shape using the template (see page 140). Allow to dry for 24 hours.

STEP 2

★ To decorate the base of the skateboard you can use a selection of edible-ink pens. You can choose any design. Here, the child's name is written in a graffiti effect. Remember to leave room for the wheels.

★ To make the skateboard wheels, roll four ⅛-inch (3 mm) black fondant balls and press with a skewer. Cut out two small black strips.

STEP 3

★ Glue the strips and wheels to the skateboard with edible glue.

★ Allow to dry and place on a frosted cupcake.

TOOLS AND MATERIALS

Knife or blade tool and a rolling pin

Blue, purple, black and orange fondants

Edible glue and brush

Black edible-ink pen

JUSTIN, THE HIPSTER

HOW TO MAKE

STEP 1

★ Roll out a ½-inch (1.5 cm) ball of orange fondant and shape into a teardrop shape.

STEP 2

★ Model a ¾-inch (2 cm) square from purple fondant to create the body. Smooth any edges with your fingers.

★ Model a black fondant square to match the body size. Use the blade tool or the back of a knife to indent for the feet.

★ Roll a blue fondant sausage shape to create the arms and cut to the correct length.

TOOLS AND MATERIALS

Knife or craft knife and rolling pin

White, red and black fondants

Black edible-ink pen

Small pearl or white ball sprinkles

Edible glue and brush

Red and yellow frosting

STEP 3

⭐ Roll out the blue fondant and cut out a 1-inch (2.5 cm) diameter circle. Use the knife to cut out the hair pattern. Glue to the head.

⭐ Assemble the parts and glue together. Once dry you can draw the face on with an edible-ink pen.

THE ROCK GUITAR

HOW TO MAKE

STEP 1

⭐ Roll out the white fondant to a ⅛ inch (3 mm) thickness and cut out the guitar shape using the template (see page 140).

⭐ Roll out the red fondant to a ⅛-inch (3 mm) thickness and use the template again to create the red Stratocaster effect. Glue to the white base.

STEP 2

⭐ Using black fondant, roll sausages as thin as you can to create three strings about 1¼-inches (3 cm) long each. Glue to the guitar body. Using two small white fondant rectangles, secure the ends of the strings.

⭐ Using a black edible-ink pen, mark the frets on the neck of the guitar.

⭐ Glue the ball sprinkles to the head of the guitar and add one at the bottom for the volume button. Allow to dry for 12 hours.

STEP 3

⭐ Place red and yellow frosting in a piping bag to create a two-tone flame effect (see page 15) and place the guitar on top.

ROCK TATTOO

We will rock you! This tattoo-inspired cake topper will hit the bass for any hardcore rocker!

TOOLS AND MATERIALS

A selection of red, gray, yellow, blue and black fondants

Knife or blade tool and a rolling pin

Black edible-ink pen

Edible silver luster or edible pearl luster spray

Silver ball sprinkles

Plastic wrap

Edible glue and brush

Toothpicks and skewers

THE WINGED HEART

HOW TO MAKE

STEP 1

★ Roll out a 2-inch (5 cm) ball of red fondant and roll into a teardrop shape. Make a cut in the top to make the heart shape. Use your fingers to smooth out the heart shape and any rough edges. Insert two skewers into the bottom of the heart.

THE GUITAR AND ROSE

STEP 2

★ Roll out the gray fondant to ¼ inch (7 mm) thick and use the template on page 141 to cut out the two wing shapes. Use your fingers to smooth out any rough edges on the wings.

★ Use the blade to mark out and indent the wing pattern.

★ Cut away the tip of the wings to produce the feather effect. Allow to dry before spraying/painting silver. When the paint is dry, glue the wings to the heart.

★ Roll out some yellow fondant. Cut a strip for the rock banner and glue in place across the heart. Once dry, write "ROCK" using black edible ink pen.

HOW TO MAKE

★ Roll out the black fondant and cut out the guitar handle using the template on page 140. Insert a toothpick into the handle, use a knife to indent the lines to represent the strings and glue silver balls to the end of the handle.

★ Roll nine ⅓-inch (8 mm) blue fondant balls. Place them between layers of plastic wrap and press each ball with your finger in an outward-circling motion to create petals. Remove the plastic wrap. Curl one of the petals around itself to create the center of the bud.

★ Now add three petals around the center and then another five petals to form a second layer. Curl the edges of the outer petal over with your finger. Trim any excess at the base.

★ Leave to dry for at least 24 hours. When all the parts are dry, assemble together on the cake.

Get the girls together and head straight for these cupcakes!

TOOLS AND MATERIALS

Knife or blade tool and rolling pin

Skewer

Black and pastel pink fondants

Edible glue and brush

THE HAIR STRAIGHTENERS

HOW TO MAKE

STEP 1

★ Roll a 2½-inch (6.5 cm) long sausage out of black fondant. Using a knife, cut the sausage almost in half lengthwise and split to create the hair straightener's shape.

STEP 2

★ Roll out a small piece of pastel pink fondant to ⅛ inch (3 mm) thick and cut out two small rectangles that are 1 inch (2.5 cm) long and glue to the hair straighteners to create the ceramic plates.

★ Indent the end of the hair straighteners with the round end of a skewer to denote the hinge.

STEP 3

★ Allow to dry for 24 hours and place on a frosted cupcake.

★ Roll a thin sausage out of black fondant to create the cord and add to the cupcake while still pliable.

TOOLS AND MATERIALS

Knife or blade tool and rolling pin

1-inch (2.5 cm) and ½-inch (1.5cm) circle cutters

Skewer

Pastel pink, hot pink and gray fondants

Edible glue and brush

THE MP3 PLAYER

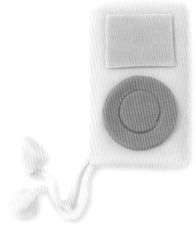

HOW TO MAKE

STEP 1

★ Roll out the pale pink fondant to ¼ inch (7 mm) thick and cut out a 2¼ x 1¼-inch (5.5 x 3 cm) rectangle. Smooth the corners with your fingers.

STEP 2

★ To make the button, roll out a small piece of hot pink fondant, cut out a 1-inch (2.5 cm) circle and then indent it with the ½-inch (1.5 cm) circle cutter.

★ Roll out a small piece of gray fondant and cut out a 1 x ¾-inch (2.5 x 2 cm) rectangle for the screen.

★ Roll two small ¼-inch (7 mm) pastel pink fondant balls and pinch the tops to create the earphones. Using a skewer, create a small hole in the tip where the wire will fit.

★ Glue the button and screen to the base and allow to dry for 24 hours.

STEP 3

★ Roll out two thin sausages to create the wires. Place the base and earphones onto a frosted cupcake and, while the fondant is still soft, position the wires from the earphones onto the back of the MP3 player.

HIPPIE CHICK

Spread peace and love with these funky hippie-chick cake and cupcakes.

TOOLS AND MATERIALS

Knife or blade tool and rolling pin

Skewer and toothpick or no.3 modeling tool

Brown, hot pink, pale pink and green fondants

Edible glue and brush

Wire

Small flower cutter

Heart cutter or heart template

2-inch (5 cm) circle cutter

⅛-inch (3 mm) circle cutter

THE OWL

HOW TO MAKE

STEP 1

★ Roll a 2-inch (5 cm) ball of brown fondant into a pear shape and pinch two ear shapes.

★ Cut two triangles from hot pink fondant and cut two slightly smaller triangles from pale pink fondant. Glue the smaller triangles to the larger triangles to make the ears.

★ Cut two hot pink fondant circles for the eyes, then cut two slightly smaller pale pink circles and two even smaller brown circles. Cut a small wedge out of the brown circles and assemble the eyes. Roll a small ball of pale pink fondant and add to the eyes.

★ Cut a green fondant triangle for the beak.

THE OWL CUPCAKE

HOW TO MAKE

★ Cut out a 2-inch (5 cm) circle from the pale pink fondant.

★ Use the template on page 141 to cut out the owl shape from brown fondant. Glue to the pink disk. Cut out a ¾-inch (2 cm) circle in brown fondant and use the cutter again to cut two wing shapes.

★ Cut two green fondant circles for the eyes and glue in place. Roll two small hot pink balls and glue to the eyes.

★ Cut a hot pink fondant triangle for the beak and glue in place.

★ Use the ⅛-inch (3 mm) circle cutter to cut pink or green fondant circles and glue around the owl.

★ Leave to dry for 24 hours.

STEP 2

★ For the feet, roll a ½-inch (1.5 cm) ball from pale pink fondant and cut in half, roll into a sausage shape and use a knife or blade tool to mark two indents for the claws.

★ Use a ⅛-inch (3 mm) circle cutter to mark the feathers across the owl's breast.

>

THE HEART

HOW TO MAKE

★ Cut out a 2-inch (5 cm) diameter circle from the brown fondant.

★ Cut out a heart from green fondant and glue to the circle.

★ Use the ⅛-inch (3 mm) circle cutter to cut hot pink fondant circles and glue around the heart.

THE BUTTERFLY

HOW TO MAKE

★ Cut a 2-inch (5 cm) diameter circle from the pale pink fondant.

★ Cut out four small hearts from the brown fondant and glue to the pink circle.

★ Cut four smaller green and pink fondant hearts and glue to the brown hearts.

★ Roll a hot pink sausage for the butterfly body and glue in place.

★ Cut three small pink balls graduating in size and stick them to the bottom of the wing. Repeat for the other wing.

THE BIRD

HOW TO MAKE

★ Cut out a 2-inch (5 cm) diameter circle from the brown fondant.

★ Use the template on page 141 to cut out a bird shape from the pale pink fondant and glue to the brown circle. Use a toothpick to mark an eye.

★ Use the 2-inch (5 cm) circle cutter to cut out the wings from brown fondant and glue in place.

★ Cut a triangle for the beak from hot pink fondant and fix in place.

★ Use the ⅛-inch (3 mm) circle cutter to cut green or pink fondant circles and glue around the bird.

THE PEACE SIGN

HOW TO MAKE

★ Cut out a 2-inch (5 cm) diameter circle from brown fondant.

★ Cut a 1¾-inch (4.5 cm) circle from pink fondant, and then cut a smaller 1¼-inch (3 cm) circle to create a ring. Glue the ring to the brown circle.

★ Take the 1¼-inch (3 cm) diameter circle, cut away four wedge sections and place into the ring, leaving you with a peace sign.

Let's all go to the lobby and get ourselves a treat!
It's time for a hot dog, popcorn or a cool, refreshing cola!

TOOLS AND MATERIALS

Small scissors

Red and white cupcake liners

Mini white marshmallows

Store-bought chocolate fudge frosting

Clear, hard candy

White sugar sprinkles

Candy stick

Pale brown, brown, yellow and red fondants

THE HOT DOG

HOW TO MAKE

STEP 1

★ Create a 1½-inch (4 cm) pale brown fondant oblong and a ¾-inch (2 cm) brown fondant wiener.

STEP 2

★ Place the ice cubes on top of the frosting and insert a candy stick to represent the drinking straw.

★ Sprinkle with white sugar sprinkles.

STEP 2

★ Cut the pale brown oblong to create the hot dog bun and insert the wiener.

THE COLA

HOW TO MAKE

STEP 1

★ Frost the cupcake with chocolate fudge frosting.

★ Using a knife, tap the hard candy to break it and create squares for ice cubes.

MARSHMALLOW POPCORN

HOW TO MAKE

STEP 1

★ Using scissors, cut slits to form a cross in the mini marshmallows.

STEP 3

★ Create the mustard by rolling a thin yellow fondant sausage and curling it on top of the hot dog along with small flecks of red fondant to represent the ketchup.

STEP 2

★ Place on top of a frosted cupcake to create a bucket of popcorn.

This cupcake creation will be perfect for watching that big game with a bunch of friends.

TOOLS AND MATERIALS

20 cupcakes baked in green liners

14 x 10 inch (35.5 x 25.5 cm) cake board

Green frosting, piping bag and Wilton no. 233 tip

White fondant

Knife or blade tool and rolling pin

Store bought soccer cake decorations to include goals and players

Toothpicks and white mailing stickers

NOTES ON THE CAKE

This cupcake selection can be made to cater for as many people as you like. Twenty cupcakes were used here, and they were placed on a 14 x 10 inch (35.5 x 25.5 cm) rectangular cake board in four rows of five. If you need to transport this cake, it's a good idea to dot a small amount of frosting on the bottom of each cupcake case, which will act as glue and keep the cupcakes in place.

SOCCER FIELD

HOW TO MAKE

STEP 1

★ Color the frosting green and place in a piping bag. Don't add a piping tip, and pipe around the entire edge of the soccer field. Then pipe over any holes between the cupcakes.

★ Now add the piping tip and start piping the grass onto the field. If you find that some cupcakes are lower than others, just infill with extra frosting and pipe grass overtop. To ensure an even field, pipe in rows.

STEP 2

★ Roll out some white fondant and cut out ¼-inch (7 mm) wide strips for the sidelines. Lay the sidelines over the grass while it is still wet.

★ Position the goal posts and players. You could also make corner flags with toothpicks and stickers.

Time to carve some killer waves with these ocean-inspired frosting effects, cracker sand and cool surfboards.

TOOLS AND MATERIALS

A selection of white and colored fondants

Knife or blade tool and rolling pin

Toothpick or skewer

Star sprinkles

¼-inch (7 mm) flower cutter/plunger

Edible glue and a brush

Black edible-ink pen

Piping bag and Wilton no.16 tip
(or a small star shape)

Blue- and white-colored
buttercream frostings

Graham cracker crumbs

NOTES ON THE CAKE

An 8-inch (20 cm) round cake covered in water-effect fondant (see page 17) was used. Cut-out waves, made from blue and white fondants were glued around the base of the cake. Applying edible glue to the top of the cake and liberally sprinkling graham cracker crumbs on top of the cake created sand. Surfboards and the sign in the sand were inserted on the top of the cake, and the flip-flops placed in front.

THE SURFBOARD

HOW TO MAKE

STEP 1

★ Roll out white fondant to ¼ inch (7 mm) thick and cut out a large surfboard shape using the template on page 140.

★ Insert a toothpick into the base of the surfboard about halfway up the toothpick.

★ Decorate the surfboards with a selection of colored fondants and sprinkles.

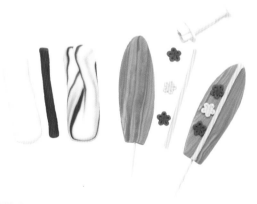

STEP 2

★ **Water-effect surfboard cake topper:**
Take a sausage shape of white fondant and add a small sausage of blue fondant. Roll together to create a long sausage and then fold together. Roll again and fold until desired water effect is achieved. Roll out to ¼ inch (7 mm) thick and cut out the large surfboard shape using the template on page 140.

★ Insert a toothpick as above and decorate with a pink strip and flowers, using a flower cutter. Secure in place with edible glue.

★ Leave to dry for at least 24 hours.

THE SURFBOARD

HOW TO MAKE

★ Follow the same instructions as you did to create the cake topper surfboards, but use the smaller surfboard template on page 141—toothpicks are not required.

★ Decorate with a selection of fondant colors and effects.

★ Leave to dry for 24 hours before frosting the cupcakes.

THE SIGN AND FLIP-FLOPS

HOW TO MAKE

★ Create an "Aloha" sign by rolling out wood-effect fondant (see page 17) to ¼ inch (7 mm) thick and cut out a sign shape using the template on page 140.

★ Make two bases for the sign and insert toothpicks through them and up into the main part of the sign.

★ After 24 hours drying, write "Aloha" in black edible ink.

★ Using a small amount of red fondant, mold two small flip-flop base shapes. Roll out some white fondant as thin as you can and glue to each side and at the center of the flip-flops.

THE CUPCAKES

HOW TO MAKE

★ Frost the cupcake with flat, white buttercream and immediately immerse in graham cracker crumbs to create the sand effect.

★ Place blue and white buttercream frosting in a piping bag with the no.16 tip. Practice a few strokes to get the correct color mix and piping effect.

★ Pipe half of the top of the cupcake with waves and then insert the surfboard cupcake topper into the sand.

PIZZA

If you are having a pizza party, why not have pizza for dessert, too?

TOOLS AND MATERIALS

Knife or craft knife and rolling pin

Ball tool and sponge

Beige fondant or marzipan (almond paste)

Pink, brown, green and yellow fondants

1-inch (2.5 cm) circle cutter

Black, red or brown edible-ink pens

Edible brown luster or paint and brush

Clear alcohol (white rum or vodka)

Yellow frosting

Seedless fruit jelly

Black jelly beans

Green sugar sprinkles

Round cake board to fit the number of cupcakes required

THE TOPPINGS

HOW TO MAKE

MUSHROOMS

★ Roll out some beige fondant or marzipan and, using a 1-inch (2.5 cm) circle cutter, cut out a circle. Use the same cutter again to create a crescent shape from the circle. Take a black edible-ink pen and mark the mushroom's gills, using the edge of the tip.

PEPPERONI

★ Roll out a mix of pink and brown fondant to ⅛ inch (3 mm) thick and cut out 1-inch (2.5 cm) diameter circles. Using a ball tool, place the circles on a sponge and indent the pepperoni. Add dots with edible red or brown ink.

HAM

★ Roll out pink fondant to ⅛ inch (3 mm) thick and cut out ¾-inch (2 cm) squares. Place on a sponge and, using a ball tool, roll the ham to create the curled corners.

GREEN PEPPERS

★ Roll out green fondant to ⅛ inch (3 mm) thick and cut out 1½-inch (4 cm) rectangles. Round the edges and bend into a boomerang shape.

PINEAPPLE

★ Roll out yellow fondant to ¼ inch (7 mm) thick and cut a rectangle shape. Using a knife, cut alternating pineapple slices. Indent with the knife.

OLIVES

★ Simply use black jelly beans.

THE PIZZA

HOW TO MAKE

★ Take your required number of cupcakes and place onto a suitably sized round cake board. Arrange them as tightly together as you can.

★ Using a piping bag and any star tip, pipe the yellow-colored frosting around the edge in a circular motion, working toward the center, until you fill the pizza. With a spoon, smooth the frosting evenly.

★ Stir the seedless jelly in a bowl to make it smoother and place in a piping bag with a star-shaped tip. Pipe the jelly around the edge of the crust to create the tomato sauce.

★ Arrange your pizza toppings on the pizza and sprinkle with green sugar to mimic oregano.

★ Take some beige fondant or marzipan and create a sausage that will form the crust. It needs to be long enough to go around the circumference of the pizza. Lay in place.

★ Mix a small amount of brown luster powder with clear alcohol and paint onto the crust with a brush to create that just-baked effect.

These delicious chicken drumsticks are presented in a fondant-decorated chicken bucket!

TOOLS AND MATERIALS

Knife or craft knife and rolling pin

White and yellow fondants

6-inch (15 cm) diameter vanilla cake or 12 vanilla cupcakes

2 cups (500 ml) of buttercream frosting

6 graham crackers

NOTES ON THE CAKE

To create the bucket-shaped cake, the cake was baked in the base of a giant cupcake pan. After a layer of frosting (see page 13), the cake was covered in red fondant, and black liquorice sticks were used to trim the top. The sides are decorated with fondant stars and a fondant chicken character. The fries box was made with card and a simple box template found online.

THE DRUMSTICKS

HOW TO MAKE

STEP 1

★ Roll out a white fondant sausage that is 2½ inches (6.5 cm) long and, using a knife, split the top and smooth the edges with your fingers to create the chicken bones.

★ To create the fries, roll out yellow fondant to ¼ inch (7 mm) thick and cut long rectangles to mimic fries. Leave to dry for 24 hours.

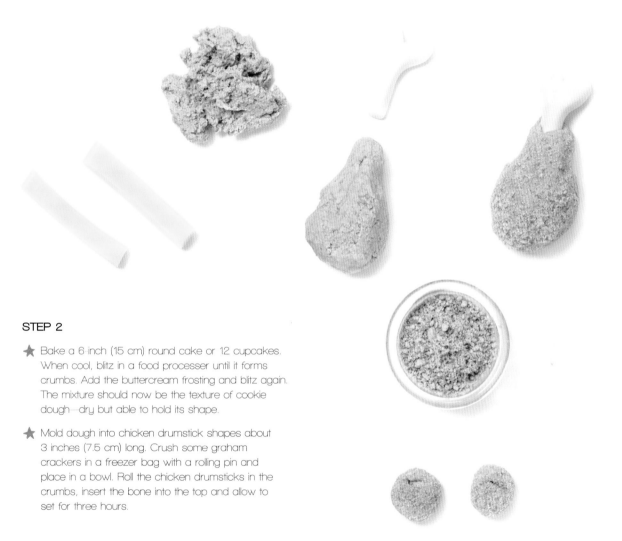

STEP 2

★ Bake a 6-inch (15 cm) round cake or 12 cupcakes. When cool, blitz in a food processer until it forms crumbs. Add the buttercream frosting and blitz again. The mixture should now be the texture of cookie dough—dry but able to hold its shape.

★ Mold dough into chicken drumstick shapes about 3 inches (7.5 cm) long. Crush some graham crackers in a freezer bag with a rolling pin and place in a bowl. Roll the chicken drumsticks in the crumbs, insert the bone into the top and allow to set for three hours.

STEP 3

★ Any leftover dough can be rolled into small balls and made into popcorn chicken.

★ Assemble the chicken on top of the cake with the fries.

Before you tee off, you might want to check that nobody's eaten the 18th hole!

TOOLS AND MATERIALS

16 cupcakes baked in green liners

14 x 10-inch (35.5 x 25.5 cm) cake board

Green-colored frosting, piping bag and Wilton no. 233 tip

Knife or blade tool and rolling pin

Water-effect and marble-effect fondant (see page 17)

Brown, green, yellow and orange fondants

Chocolate cookie finger pretzel stick

5 graham crackers and Oreo cookies

Store bought golfer cake decoration

Edible glue and brush

NOTES ON THE CAKE

This cupcake selection can be made for as many people as you like. Sixteen cupcakes on a 14 x 10-inch (35.5 x 25.5 cm) cake board were used here.

THE DECORATIONS

HOW TO MAKE

ROCKS

★ Use the technique on page 17 to create marble-effect fondant and mold it into rocks.

TREES

★ Roll out a 1-inch (2.5 cm) ball of green fondant and mold into a cone. With scissors, snip the cone to create branches, starting at the top and working your way down. You can the insert a chocolate cookie finger or pretzel stick to create the trunk. Repeat to make additional trees and bushes of various sizes. Leave to dry for 24 hours.

BRIDGE

★ Roll out the brown fondant to ¼ inch (7 mm) thick and cut out two strips that are ¼ x 3¼ inches (7 mm x 8.5 cm). Roll out the brown fondant again to ⅛ inch (3 mm) thick and cut out a 1 x 3-inch (2.5 x 7.5 cm) rectangle.

★ Lay the bridge base over a rolling pin and glue the bridge sides in place. Using a knife, mark the sides to look like bricks. Leave to dry for 24 hours.

DUCK

★ Roll two balls of yellow fondant that are ¼-inch (7 mm) and ½-inch (1 cm). Mold the larger ball as the duck's body along with the tail. Glue the head in place and add eyes with a toothpick. Mold a small beak from orange fondant and glue in place.

THE COURSE

HOW TO MAKE

STEP 1

★ Plan where you want to put the green, 18th hole, bunkers, river, dirt and grass.

★ Place five graham crackers in a plastic freezer bag and crush them with a rolling pin. Frost the cupcakes for the bunkers and dip them into the cracker sand.

STEP 2

★ Roll out the green fondant to ¼ inch (7 mm) thick and cut out the first hole and 18th green. Frost the cupcakes and lay the fondant in place. Create a hole on the 18th green with a toothpick.

★ Use the technique on page 17 to create water-effect fondant. Roll to ¼ inch (7 mm) thick and cut out the river. You will need to frost the cupcakes where the river will flow and lay in place.

STEP 3

★ Color the buttercream frosting green and place in a piping bag with a Wilton no. 233 tip and start piping the grass onto the remainder of the course. If you find that some cupcakes are lower than others, just infill with extra frosting and pipe grass overtop.

★ Finally, add the rocks around the river and put the bridge in place. You can also add the duck, a store-bought golfer and an 18th hole flag (made from a toothpick and white sticker).

★ Using the same technique as for sand, crush five Oreo cookies (remove the cream first) to create dirt. Frost the desired cupcakes, dunk in "dirt" and add the trees.

If you know your jack saw from your hacksaw, these DIY-themed cupcakes are the ones for you!

TOOLS AND MATERIALS

Knife or craft knife and rolling pin

Blade tool

Gray, black and yellow fondants

Black edible-ink pen

Toothpick

Edible glue and brush

THE HAMMER

HOW TO MAKE

STEP 1

★ Using gray fondant, roll out a ¾-inch (2 cm) long sausage shape for the hammerhead.

★ Roll out a thin yellow fondant sausage to create the neck and a black fondant sausage for the handle.

STEP 2

★ Mark the black handle with a toothpick to create a dimpled effect.

★ Using a blade tool, indent the head of the hammer and create a split to make the claw of the hammerhead.

STEP 3

★ Glue together and allow to dry for 24 hours before placing on top of a frosted cupcake.

THE TAPE MEASURE

HOW TO MAKE

STEP 1

★ Roll out a ½-inch (1 cm) ball of yellow fondant and press with your finger to create a ¼-inch (7 mm) diameter round.

★ Roll out a ¼-inch (7 mm) ball of black fondant and press with your finger to create a circle that will cover the yellow round. Cut a black rectangle that is ¼-inch (7 mm) wide that you can glue three-quarters of the way around the edge of the yellow round.

STEP 2

★ Cut a rectangle from yellow fondant that is ¼ inch (7 mm) by 1 inch (2.5 cm) to create the tape. Cut out a small gray fondant rectangle to cover the end of the tape measure.

STEP 3

★ Glue the tape measure to the base of the round.

★ Allow to dry for 24 hours before placing on top of a frosted cupcake.

THE SAW

HOW TO MAKE

STEP 1

★ Roll out the gray fondant to a thickness of ⅛ inch (3 mm) and cut out the saw shape using the template (see page 140). Using the tip of the craft knife, create teeth on the cutting edge of the saw.

STEP 2

★ Roll out the black fondant to a thickness of ⅛ inch (3 mm) and cut out the saw handle shape using the template (see page 140). Glue the handle to the blade.

STEP 3

★ Allow to dry for 24 hours and place on a frosted cupcake.

Ideal for those loved ones with green thumbs— this lush green hideaway is a gardener's treat!

TOOLS AND MATERIALS

Knife or blade tool and rolling pin

Toothpicks

Gray, green, brown, red, tan, stone and yellow fondants

Three graham crackers

Five Oreo cookies

Freezer bag

15 cupcakes baked in brown liners

14 x 10-inch (35.5 x 25.5 cm) cake board

Green-colored frosting

Piping bag and Wilton no.233 tip

Plain frosting

¼-inch (7 mm) flower cutter

Edible glue and brush

NOTES ON THE CAKE

This cupcake selection can be made for as many people as you like. In this case, 15 cupcakes were used and placed on a 14 x 10-inch (35.5 x 25.5 cm) rectangular cake board. If you need to transport this cake, dot a small amount of frosting to the bottom of each cupcake to act as glue and keep them in place.

THE WATERING CAN

HOW TO MAKE

STEP 1

★ Mold the body of the watering can from a 1½-inch (4 cm) ball of gray fondant, with a taper at the top. Using a blade tool, mark the two rings around the bottom, and one at the top.

★ With a ¼-inch (7 mm) ball of gray fondant, roll a sausage shape to create the spout. Ensure that the base has a diagonal so it will fit the body of the watering can.

STEP 2

★ Roll out the gray fondant to ⅛ inch (3 mm) thick and cut a 1 x ¼-inch (2.5 cm x 7 mm) strip for the side handle. Curl it on its side to make a question-mark shape. Cut a smaller strip for the top handle. Again, curl it on its side in a half-moon shape. Leave to dry for 10 minutes before gluing the parts onto the body of the watering can.

★ Leave to dry for 24 hours before placing on the cake.

THE STEPPING STONES

HOW TO MAKE

★ Roll out some stone effect fondant (see page 17), using tan and white fondant, to ¼ inch (7 mm) thick and cut out seven ¾ inch (2 cm) squares. Leave to dry for 24 hours.

THE HOSEPIPE

HOW TO MAKE

★ Roll out a thin, long sausage of green fondant and curl it around itself to create the hose. Add a gray and yellow fondant nozzle with glue. Leave to dry and then gently place on the cake.

THE FLOWERPOTS

HOW TO MAKE

★ Mix some brown and red fondants to create a terra-cotta color. Roll it out to ⅛ inch (3 mm) thick and cut out a ¾-inch (2 cm) wide strip. Wrap it around a metal piping tip for the flowerpot shape and trim the edges.

★ Cut out a ½-inch (1 cm) diameter circle and glue to the base. Pierce the bottom with a skewer to create the hole.

★ Cut another strip that is ⅛ inch (3 mm) wide and glue in place to be the rim of the pot.

THE RUBBER BOOTS

HOW TO MAKE

★ Roll a 1½-inch (4 cm) ball of green fondant and mold it into one wide rubber boot. Using a blade tool, score down the middle to create two boots (but do not separate them!). Then, using the same tool, create a heel and imprint the tread on the sole. Leave to dry for 24 hours and place on the cake.

THE TREES AND BUSHES

HOW TO MAKE

★ Roll out a 1-inch (2.5 cm) ball of green fondant and mold into a cone. With scissors, snip the cone to create branches, starting at the top and working your way down. Insert a toothpick into the base so you will be able to place it in the cake. Repeat to make additional trees and bushes of various sizes. Leave to dry for 24 hours.

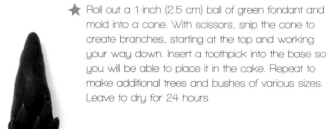

ASSEMBLE THE GARDEN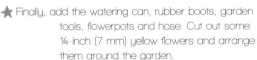

HOW TO MAKE

PATH

★ Place three graham crackers in a freezer bag and crush with a rolling pin. The crumbs should resemble sand. Frost the path across the cupcakes and sprinkle the graham crackers over the frosting. Pat with your finger to secure. Add the stepping stones.

DIRT

★ Use the same technique as for the path, but crush five Oreo cookies (remove the cream first) to create the dirt. Frost the desired cupcakes, dunk them in the "dirt," and add the trees and flowers.

GRASS

★ Color the frosting green and place in a piping bag with a Wilton no. 233 grass tip and start piping the grass onto the remainder of the garden. If you find that some cupcakes are lower than others, just infill with extra frosting and pipe grass overtop.

★ Finally, add the watering can, rubber boots, garden tools, flowerpots and hose. Cut out some ¼-inch (7 mm) yellow flowers and arrange them around the garden.

THE GARDEN TOOLS

HOW TO MAKE

★ Roll out the gray fondant to ⅛ inch (3 mm) thick and cut out a small "U" shape. Trim the top to create the fork prongs.

★ Roll out a thin sausage of gray fondant and cut the top section in two. Glue the fork into the recess. Add a thin sausage of tan fondant to the base to create a handle.

★ Repeat the process for the trowel, but do not cut prongs into the top.

★ Leave to dry for 24 hours before placing on the cake.

These cake toppers encompass all of a girl's favorite pastimes—shopping, shoes and dresses!

TOOLS AND MATERIALS

Knife or blade tool and rolling pin

Pale pink, hot pink, black and white fondants

2¼-inch (5.5 cm) circle cutter

¼-inch (7 mm) and ⅓-inch (8 mm) circle cutters

⅛-inch (3 mm) flower cutter

Small star cutter

Star sprinkles

Small amount of paper towel

Edible glue and brush

NOTES ON THE CAKE

An 8-inch (20 cm) square cake covered in pale pink fondant was used. A black border and black vertical stripes were added for decoration. The bags and boxes were arranged around the top, and the black dress was draped over the edge.

THE SHOPPING BAG

HOW TO MAKE

STEP 1

★ Roll out the pale pink fondant to ⅛-inch (3 mm) thick. Cut out the following shapes:

Two 2 x 1½-inch (5 x 4 cm) rectangles to form the front and back of the bag.

One ¾ x 2-inch (2 x 5 cm) rectangle to form base of the bag.

Two ¾ x 1½-inch (2 x 4 cm) rectangles to form the sides of the bag.

★ Using a knife tool, score the two side panels with a "Y," as this will allow you to bend the fondant.

★ Leave the parts to dry for 20 minutes. This will allow you to assemble the parts without them flopping around.

STEP 2

★ Once dry, glue all the sides and assemble together. Place a sheet of paper towel in the bag to help it keep its shape.

★ Roll out a small piece of black fondant and cut a thin strip that is 1½ inch (4 cm) long. While wet, shape into a handle and glue on a string of pearl ball sprinkles. While still wet, attach to the front of the bag.

STEP 3

★ Roll out some white fondant as thinly as you can, cut out a rectangle, ruffle it and add to the inside of the bag to create tissue paper.

★ Leave to dry for 24 hours and place on the cake. You can use this technique to make other sized bags and add different decorations, as was done with the blossom bag.

>

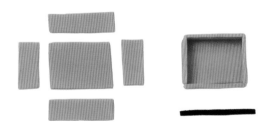

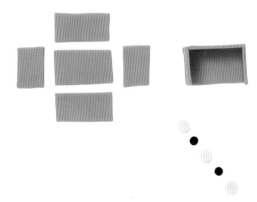

THE SHOEBOX

HOW TO MAKE

STEP 1

★ Roll out the hot pink fondant to ⅛ inch (3 mm) thick and cut out the following shapes:

LID

- One 2 x 1½-inch (5 x 4 cm) rectangle for the lid top.
- Two 2 x 1½-inch (5 x 4 cm) rectangles for the long sides.
- Two 1½ x ½-inch (4 x 1 cm) rectangles for the short sides.

BASE

- One 2 x 1-inch (5 x 2.5 cm) rectangle for the base.
- Two 2 x ¾-inch (5 x 2 cm) rectangles for the long sides.
- Two 1 x ¾-inch (2.5 x 2 cm) rectangles for the short sides.

★ Leave the parts to dry for 20 minutes. This will allow you to assemble the parts without them flopping around.

★ Once dry, glue all the sides and assemble.

STEP 2

★ Roll out a small amount of black fondant and cut thin strips to decorate the lid and sides of the box. Glue in place.

★ Cut out small ¼-inch (7 mm) black circles and ⅓-inch (8 mm) pale pink circles and decorate the lid of the box. Add some tissue-paper fondant (made in the same way as for the shopping bag), and glue in place. Leave to dry for 24 hours before placing on the cake.

THE SHOE

HOW TO MAKE

★ Using black fondant, mold a shoe. Use a small ball to form the sole and lay it over a pencil to dry to give the arch effect. After leaving to dry for an hour, form a heel, back and toe strap and glue in place. The shoes are painted with confectioners' glaze to make them shine and give a patent effect. Leave to dry before placing on the cake.

THE HATBOX

HOW TO MAKE

STEP 1

★ Roll out the white fondant to ⅛ inch (3 mm) thick and cut out the following parts:

LID

- One 2¼-inch (5.5 cm) diameter circle.
- One 6 x ⅓-inch (15 cm x 8 mm) rectangular strip for the edge.

BASE

- One 1 x 6-inch (15 x 2.5 cm) rectangle.

STEP 2

★ To form the lid, glue the edge strip to the sides of the circle. Leave to dry.

★ To form the base, curl the rectangle around a 2¼-inch (5.5 cm) circle cutter, leave to dry for 24 hours and then remove the cutter.

STEP 3

★ Roll out the black fondant and cut ⅛-inch (3 mm) strips to decorate the rim of the lid, laying them diagonally across the top and vertically around the base. Glue in place and leave to dry for 24 hours.

★ Add some tissue-paper fondant (as for the shopping bag) and place on the cake.

THE BLACK DRESS

HOW TO MAKE

STEP 1

★ Once all the cake toppers are in place on the cake, roll out the black fondant and, using the large dress template on page 141, cut out the dress shape.

STEP 2

★ Add a belt and corsage, using a ⅛ inch (3 mm) flower cutter, and glue onto the dress. While still wet, drape over the hatbox. You may need to add some black fondant to the back to provide support.

THE SHOE

HOW TO MAKE

★ Roll out the black and hot pink fondants to ⅛ inch (3 mm) thick and cut out a shoe shape using the template on page 141.

★ Cut a small square off each heel, change them over and glue in place.

★ Leave to dry for 24 hours and place on a frosted cupcake.

THE DRESS

HOW TO MAKE

★ Roll out the black fondant to ⅛ inch (3 mm) thick and cut out a dress shape using the small dress template on page 141.

★ Add a belt and flower corsage, using a ⅛-inch (3 mm) flower cutter, and glue onto the dress.

★ Leave to dry for 24 hours and place on a frosted cupcake.

LUAU DANCER

Have your guests hulaing to the buffet table to grab some Polynesian-inspired delights!

TOOLS AND MATERIALS

Mini doll pick

Knife or blade tool and rolling pin

Skewer and toothpick

Hot pink, yellow, orange, skin-colored and pale gold fondants

Two marshmallows

1¼-inch (3 cm) circle cutter

2½-inch (6.5 cm) flower cutter

Ball tool

Foam pad and forming cup

Edible-ink pen or paintbrush and food coloring

Edible glue and paintbrush

⅛-inch (3 mm) flower cutter

Shredded wheat

NOTES ON THE CAKE

An 8-inch (20 cm) round cake covered in tan fondant was used. The sides have been decorated with chocolate wafer rolls to give the "tiki hut" effect. Graham cracker crumbs were glued to the top, and the edges were decorated with small flowers and fondant shells sprayed with gold luster.

LUAU DANCER

HOW TO MAKE

STEP 1

★ Insert the marshmallows onto a skewer and your doll pick into the top of the marshmallows.

★ Gently break off some of the shredded wheat and glue to the marshmallow skirt.

LUAU DANCER

STEP 2

★ Cut out a 1¼-inch (3 cm) hot pink fondant circle, cut a smaller circle from the middle and cut open the back to make the waistband. Glue in place to cover any untidy edges. Cut out a bikini shape and glue to the doll.

STEP 3

★ Use the skin-colored fondant to mold the legs to suit the size of your doll, gently push the skewer through the legs, then remove and leave the legs to dry for 24 hours.

STEP 4

★ Using the small flower cutter, cut out the flowers in orange, yellow and pink fondant for the lei. Mark the center of each flower with the edible-ink pen or paint with the food coloring. Glue the flowers in place.

★ Repeat the process with the medium flower cutter for the hair, waist and cake decorations.

POLYNESIAN FLOWER CUPCAKE

HOW TO MAKE

STEP 1

★ Roll out one of the fondant colors and cut out a flower using the large flower cutter.

★ Place the flower on a foam pad and gently rub the ball tool around the petal edges to thin and curl.

★ Place the flower onto a forming cup.

STEP 2

★ You can paint the center of the flower with either an edible-ink pen or a little food coloring. If using a coloring paste, try mixing with a little vodka or other clear spirit first.

★ Use a contrasting color to make the stigma: roll some fondant into a thin sausage, cut it to length, and stick in place. Leave to dry for 24 hours.

If you want to make someone feel better—why not give them a basket of fruit? A sweeter version!

TOOLS AND MATERIALS

Knife or blade tool and rolling pin

Almond paste (or fondant can be substituted)

Green, orange, red, yellow and purple food coloring paste

Brown fondant

Serrated cone tool

3-inch (7.5 cm) and 2½-inch (6.5 cm) circle cutters

½-inch (1 cm) star cutter

Toothpick

Edible glue and brush

Two cupcakes in each color baked in green, orange, red, yellow and purple liners

Four mini cupcakes

Two plain cupcakes

Black edible-ink pen

NOTES ON THE BASKET

A wicker basket is used to present the almond-paste fruit cupcakes. The base of the basket is lined with tissue paper and the cupcakes are placed inside. The grapes and bananas are laid on purple and yellow almond-paste, flat-frosted cupcakes.

THE APPLE

HOW TO MAKE

★ Mix the almond paste with red coloring paste until you reach the desired color. Roll it out to ⅛ inch (3 mm) thick and cut out a 3-inch (7.5 cm) circle.

★ Remove a cupcake from its liner, slice it in half through the middle, turn it upside-down and cut four wedges and a hole from the center. Attach to the top of a cupcake baked in a red cupcake liner. Then cover the entire cupcake in frosting.

★ Lay the red fondant circle overtop and gently smooth down to create an apple shape.

★ Using a serrated cone tool or skewer, indent the top to form a small hole. Roll out a small amount of brown fondant, cut out a ½-inch (1 cm) star and place it into the hole.

THE PEAR

HOW TO MAKE

★ Mix the almond paste with green coloring paste until you reach the desired color. Roll it out to ⅛ inch (3 mm) thick and cut out a 2½-inch (1 cm) circle.

★ Place a mini cupcake on top of a cupcake baked in a green liner. Cover with frosting and then lay the green almond paste overtop and gently smooth down to create the pear shape. Using a serrated cone tool or skewer, indent the top to form a small hole. Using a knife, indent some small lines coming outward. Roll out a small amount of brown fondant and cut out a ½-inch (1 cm) star and place into the hole.

★ Take a small piece of brown fondant, mold a stalk and imprint the top with the serrated cone tool or a skewer. Glue into the hole at the top of the pear.

THE ORANGE

HOW TO MAKE

★ Mix the almond paste with a small amount of orange coloring paste until you reach the desired color. Roll it out to ⅛ inch (3 mm) thick and cut out a 2½-inch (1 cm) circle.

★ Place a tablespoon (15 ml) of frosting on top of a cupcake baked in an orange liner. Lay the orange fondant circle over the top and gently smooth down to create an orange shape.

★ Using a serrated cone tool or skewer, indent the top to form a small hole. Roll out a small amount of green fondant, cut out a ½-inch (1 cm) star and glue it into the hole.

★ Using a toothpick, indent small holes all over the orange to create a peel effect.

THE BANANAS

HOW TO MAKE

★ Mix the almond paste with yellow coloring paste until you reach the desired color. Roll a sausage about ¾ inch (2 cm) thick and 6 inches (15 cm) long.

★ To form the banana, pinch the top to make the stalk. Use your fingers along the length to mold the ridges of the banana. Using a serrated cone tool or skewer, imprint the top of the stalk. Repeat four times to make a bunch of bananas. Leave to dry for 24 hours.

★ When dry, you can draw the markings on the banana with a black edible-ink pen, along the ridges at the tip and the stalk.

THE GRAPES

HOW TO MAKE

★ Mix the almond paste with purple coloring paste until you reach the desired color. Roll out a long sausage about ¾ inch (2 cm) thick and cut off ¾-inch (2 cm) pieces. Roll each piece into individual grapes and taper the tops slightly.

★ Arrange the grapes into a bunch pattern and glue into place.

★ Take a small piece of brown fondant, mold a stalk and imprint the top with the serrated cone tool or a skewer. Glue into a gap at the top of the bunch of grapes. You can also paint the finished grapes with confectioners' glaze to make them glossy. Leave to dry for 24 hours.

These sunny flowers will brighten anyone's
day and are a perfect way to say thank you!

TOOLS AND MATERIALS

6-inch (15 cm) polystyrene craft ball

6-inch (15 cm) diameter plant pot

16 cupcakes baked in brown liners

Floral tape or a hot glue gun

Colorful tissue paper

Piping bag with white frosting and a
Wilton 1M/2110 tip

Piping bag with yellow frosting and a
Wilton no. 352 tip

16 1¼-inch (3 cm) round chocolate mints

Toothpicks

THE SUNFLOWER
BOUQUET

HOW TO MAKE

STEP 1

★ Fix a 6-inch (15 cm) polystyrene craft ball into a
suitably sized plant pot, either by taping or using a
hot glue gun. (You can cover the craft ball in a colorful
tissue paper if required before securing.)

STEP 2

★ Starting at the top and in the center, insert a
toothpick to secure the first cupcake. Now work
around and insert six more cupcakes and then a
final ring around the bottom.

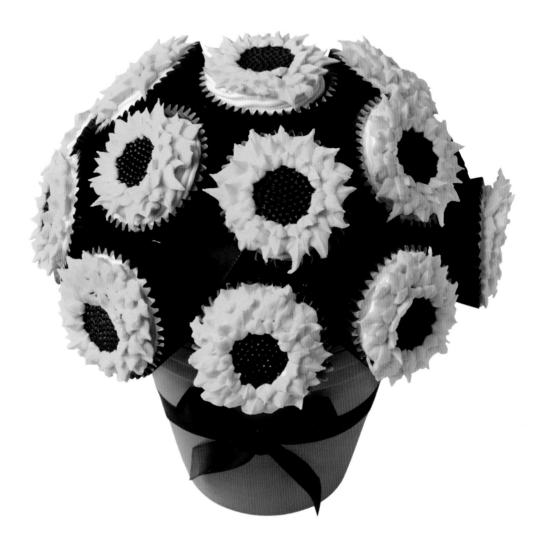

STEP 3

★ Take a cupcake off, pipe a single layer of frosting and insert a round chocolate mint in the center. Now pipe the yellow petals using the no. 352 piping tip. Pipe a ring of petals around the edge of the chocolate. Then pipe a second ring and a third.

★ Return the cupcake to the bouquet and repeat the process until all the cupcakes are piped. Add more toothpicks to secure any loose cupcakes.

A cupcake can be decorated with almost anything; these cakes are ideal for artists, needle-crafters and for special occasions.

TOOLS AND MATERIALS

Knife or craft knife and rolling pin

White, hot pink, pink, tan, yellow and gray fondants

Skewer

Edible glue and brush

THE PALETTE

HOW TO MAKE

STEP 1

★ To create the paintbrush, roll a sausage of hot pink fondant that is 1 inch (2.5 cm) long with a pointed end. To the flat end add a small ball of yellow fondant.

★ To create the bristles, roll a small ball of gray fondant and add an even smaller ball of hot pink. Pinch between your fingers to create a cone shape. Indent with a knife to create a bristle effect. Glue to the top of the paintbrush.

STEP 2

★ Roll out the white fondant to a thickness of ⅛ inch (3 mm) and cut out the artist's palette using the template (see page 140). Using the skewer, create the thumbhole.

STEP 3

★ To make the gradating paint effect, start with a small white ball of fondant and pinch it with your fingers to look like a drip of paint. Then mix the white and hot pink fondants to create different shades and finish with a hot pink drip. Glue to the palette and add the paintbrush.

★ Allow to dry and place on a frosted cupcake.

THE SEWING KIT

HOW TO MAKE

STEP 1

★ To make the spool of thread take a ½-inch (1 cm) ball of tan fondant and mold a cylinder shape that is ½ inch (1 cm) long.

★ Roll two ¼-inch (7 mm) balls of tan fondant and flatten them with your finger to create the ends of the spool. Glue in place.

STEP 2

★ Take a ½-inch (1 cm) ball of pink fondant and roll it into a long sausage, as thin as you can make it. Wrap around the spool to create a thread effect. Leave the end to curl.

STEP 3

★ To make the buttons, roll ⅓-inch (8 mm) balls in hot pink and yellow fondants and flatten with your finger. Use a skewer to indent the buttonholes.

★ To make the needle, roll a ¼-inch (7 mm) ball of gray fondant into a sausage with a point. Curl the other end over and secure with glue to create the eye of the needle.

★ Allow to dry and carefully place on a frosted cupcake.

TOOLS AND MATERIALS

Knife or blade tool and rolling pin
....
2½-inch (6.5 cm) heart-shaped cutter
....
Toothpick and skewer
....
Black and pale yellow fondant
....
Gold edible paint
....
Gold edible luster spray
....
Gold edible glitter
....
¼-inch (7 mm) flower cutter
....
Black nonpareils
....
Edible glue and brush

THE MASKS

HOW TO MAKE

STEP 1

★ Roll out the black fondant (or gold for the gold mask) to a thickness of ⅛-inch (3 mm) and cut out a large heart shape. Use the cutter again to cut away the top as shown.

★ Using a knife, cut out two eyeholes. Using a skewer, gently press the fondant to create a nose.

★ Gently lay over a rolling pin and allow to dry for 24 hours.

STEP 2

★ **For the black mask:** Using edible gold paint, design a curly decoration on the mask. Sprinkle with gold edible glitter. Allow to dry and place on a frosted cupcake.

★ **For the gold mask:** Using edible gold spray, cover the mask. Allow to dry and, using black food coloring, paint swirls on the mask. Roll out a small piece of black fondant and cut out two flowers. Glue black nonpareils to the center of the flowers and glue them to the mask. Sprinkle with gold edible glitter. Allow to dry and place on a frosted cupcake.

CELEBRATIONS AND THANK YOUS

Say thanks, celebrate a new home or show your appreciation for a teacher with these cupcake designs.

TOOLS AND MATERIALS

Knife or blade tool and rolling pin

Black, stone, green and yellow fondants

Marble fondant (mix white and black to create a marbled effect)

Toothpick and skewer

Edible glue and brush

THE NEW HOME

HOW TO MAKE

STEP 1

★ Roll out the black fondant to a thickness of ⅛ inch (3 mm) and cut out a rectangle that is ¾ x 1½ inch (2 x 4 cm).

★ Cut out three marble fondant rectangles to surround the black door. Make the top larger and cut the edges to a point to create the lintel.

STEP 2

★ Using the blade tool, indent the door with two rectangles and two squares. Also mark the lintel with four horizontal lines.

★ Roll out the marble fondant and cut out a rectangle and flowerpots as shown.

★ Roll out a ½-inch (1 cm) ball of green fondant and cut in two. Using the toothpick, fluff the green fondant to create bushes.

STEP 3

★ Using a small amount of yellow fondant, cut out a rectangle for the letterbox and indent. Roll a small piece of yellow between your fingers and create a knocker, add a ball of fondant to the join.

★ Glue the components together and allow to dry for 24 hours. Place on a frosted cupcake.

TOOLS AND MATERIALS

Knife or craft knife and rolling pin

Red, green, black, white and yellow fondants

Skewer

Edible glue and brush

THE CHALKBOARD

HOW TO MAKE

STEP 1

★ Roll out black fondant to a thickness of ⅛ inch (3 mm) and cut out a rectangle that is 1 x 1½ inches (2.5 x 4 cm).

★ Roll out white fondant to ⅛ inch (3 mm) thick and cut out a long thin strip that is ⅛-inch (3 mm) wide.

THE APPLES AND CRAYONS

HOW TO MAKE

STEP 1

★ To create the apple, roll a ¼-inch (7 mm) ball of red fondant and add a small ball of green fondant. Roll out another small piece of green fondant and cut out two small leaves.

★ With a small ball of black fondant, create a stalk.

★ Using a skewer, indent the top of the apple. Glue in the leaves first and then the stalk.

STEP 2

★ Using edible glue, paint the numbers 1, 2 and 3 onto the chalkboard and then lay the white fondant strip in place over the numbers, trimming any excess.

STEP 3

★ Roll a sausage of white fondant that is ¾-inch (2 cm) long to create the chalk. Allow to dry and place on a frosted cupcake.

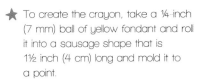

STEP 2

★ To create the crayon, take a ¼-inch (7 mm) ball of yellow fondant and roll it into a sausage shape that is 1½ inch (4 cm) long and mold it to a point.

STEP 3

★ Roll out a small amount of black fondant into the thinnest sausage you can. Glue two strips of this around the crayon at both ends.

★ Take another small ball of black fondant and mold an oblong about ¾ inch (2 cm) long to create the crayon's label. Glue in place.

★ Repeat the process to make a green crayon.

★ Allow to dry and place on a frosted cupcake.

There's no need to bluff with these casino-themed cupcakes. They're the real deal!

TOOLS AND MATERIALS

Plastic cocktail glass

Knife or craft knife and rolling pin

Red, green, white and black fondants

1½-inch (4 cm) circle cutter

¾-inch (2 cm) circle cutter

1-inch (2.5 cm) circle cutter

Black edible-ink pen

Edible glue and brush

Clear hard candies

Candy sticks

Green and white sugar sprinkles

THE DICE

HOW TO MAKE

STEP 1

★ Roll out the white fondant to ¾ inch (2 cm) thick and cut out two ¾-inch (2 cm) cubes.

★ Sharpen the edges by pinching with your fingers.

STEP 2

★ While the fondant is still wet, use the black edible-ink pen to mark the dots on the dice.

STEP 3

★ Allow to dry and place on a frosted cupcake along with green sugar sprinkles.

THE POKER CHIPS

HOW TO MAKE

STEP 1

★ Roll the red fondant out to a thickness of ¼ inch (7 mm) and, using a 1½-inch (4 cm) circle cutter, cut out a circle. Indent the chip with a ¾-inch (2 cm) circle cutter.

STEP 2

★ Roll out the black fondant to a thickness of ⅛ inch (3 mm) and cut out a 1½-inch (4 cm) diameter circle. From the circle's center cut out another ¾-inch (2 cm) circle.

★ Cut this black ring into eight equal segments. Take four of these segments and glue them to the outer ring of the red fondant chip.

★ Repeat the whole process with green fondant to create a green chip.

THE COCKTAIL

HOW TO MAKE

STEP 1

★ To make the lime slice, roll out the green fondant to ⅛ inch (3 mm) thick and, using a 1½-inch (4 cm) circle cutter, cut out a circle. Using the 1-inch (2.5 cm) cutter, indent an inner ring and, using a knife, draw lines for the pulp. Allow to dry for 24 hours.

STEP 2

★ Paint edible glue around the rim of the cupcake liner and dunk into a pile of white sugar sprinkles. Frost the cupcake with green frosting.

STEP 3

★ Cut some clear hard candies with a knife to create ice. Add to the frosted cupcake along with a candy stick for a straw and the lime slice.

★ Place the cupcake in the plastic cocktail glass to present.

STEP 3

★ Allow to dry and place on a frosted cupcake along with green sugar sprinkles.

These vintage-style cupcakes are a superb addition to any festival or celebration.

TOOLS AND MATERIALS

Knife or blade tool and rolling pin

Red, white and blue fondants

2½-inch (6.5 cm), 2-inch (5 cm) and 1-inch (2.5 cm) circle cutters

Toothpick or skewer

2¼-inch (5.5 cm), 1½-inch (4 cm), ¾-inch (2 cm) and ½-inch (1 cm) star cutters

Red, white and blue star sprinkles

White nonpareils

Edible glue and brush

THE ROSETTE

HOW TO MAKE

STEP 1

★ Roll out the red fondant and cut out a 2½-inch (6.5 cm) diameter circle. Use a ½-inch (1.5 cm) star cutter to cut out a star. Also, cut out a 2 x ½-inch (5 x 1.5 cm) rectangle and cut out a triangle from one end.

★ Roll out the blue fondant and cut out a 2-inch (5 cm) diameter circle and a ribbon as above.

★ Roll out the white fondant and cut out a 1-inch (2.5 cm) circle and another ribbon as above.

STEP 2

★ Take a skewer and place it over the edge of the red and blue circles and gently roll up and down, to create the frill detail (see page 19 for technique).

STEP 3

★ Glue the components together and allow to dry for 24 hours. Place on a frosted cupcake.

THE TRIPLE STAR

HOW TO MAKE

STEP 1

★ Roll out the three fondant colors and cut out a 2¼-inch (5.5 cm) star from the red fondant, a 1½-inch (4 cm) star from the white fondant and a ¾-inch (2 cm) star from blue fondant.

STEP 2

★ Glue together and allow to dry for 24 hours. Place on a frosted cupcake.

THE FLAGS

HOW TO MAKE

STEP 1

★ Cut out triangle shapes from blue and white fondant.

STEP 2

★ Glue onto a red flat-frosted cupcake.

★ Glue red, white and blue star sprinkles onto the flags.

STEP 3

★ Glue white nonpareils along the top of the bunting.

You will find yourself hopping crazy for these cute Easter cupcakes!

TOOLS AND MATERIALS

Knife or craft knife and rolling pin

Pastel green, blue, yellow, pink, orange and hot pink fondants

¼-inch (7 mm) circle cutter

Black edible-ink pen

Edible glue and brush

Jelly beans

THE EGGS

HOW TO MAKE

STEP 1

★ Roll out the pale green fondant to ⅛ inch (3 mm) thick and cut out an egg shape using the template (see page 140).

★ Using a ¼-inch (7 mm) circle cutter, cut out five circles in a selection of pastel colors.

STEP 2

★ Glue the circles randomly to the egg, ensuring that some cross over the edge, trimming the excess.

★ When dried, place on top of a frosted cupcake.

THE CHICKS

HOW TO MAKE

STEP 1

★ Roll out the pale yellow fondant to a thickness of ⅛ inch (3 mm) and cut out the egg shape using the template (see page 140).

★ Roll a ⅓-inch (8 mm) ball of yellow fondant, flatten with your finger and cut in two to create wings.

STEP 2

★ Glue the wings to the sides of the chick's body.

★ Cut out a small orange triangle to create the beak and glue in place.

STEP 3

★ Mark the chick's eyes with a black edible ink.

★ When dried, place on top of a frosted cupcake.

THE BUNNY

HOW TO MAKE

STEP 1

★ Roll out the pale pink fondant to a thickness of ⅛ inch (3 mm) and cut out two bunny shapes using the template (see page 140).

STEP 2

★ Take one of the bunny cutouts and cut halfway across the head to create the bunny's feet.

★ Roll a small hot pink ball of fondant and glue in place for the bunny's nose. Mark the bunny's eyes with black edible ink.

★ Create a carrot by cutting out a small triangle of orange fondant and adding a green fondant serrated top.

STEP 3

★ When dried, assemble the head and feet on a frosted cupcake along with jelly beans at his belly and the carrot.

It's Halloween! Beware this spooky witch doesn't cast a spell on you! And watch out for the ghost!

TOOLS AND MATERIALS

Knife or blade tool and rolling pin

Black, green, orange and purple fondants

Edible glue and brush

THE WITCH'S HAT

THE WITCH'S LEGS

HOW TO MAKE

STEP 1

★ Roll out the black fondant and cut out two witch's boots using the template on page 140.

STEP 2

★ Roll the purple and green fondant into ¼-inch (7 mm) wide sausages. Cut the sausages into ¼-inch (7 mm) pieces.

★ Glue the pieces back together in alternating colors to make the witch's legs, which should be about 3 inches (7.5 cm) long.

HOW TO MAKE

STEP 1

★ Roll a 1-inch (2.5 cm) ball of black fondant and mold the top into the point of the hat.

STEP 2

★ Roll out the black fondant to ⅛ inch (3 mm) thick and cut out a 1½-inch (4 cm) circle.

STEP 3

★ Glue together the circle and hat point and allow to dry for 24 hours. Place on a frosted cupcake.

STEP 3

★ Glue the witch's boots to the legs and allow to dry for 24 hours.

★ Insert into a frosted cupcake.

THE GHOST

HOW TO MAKE

STEP 1

★ From a 1½-inch (4 cm) white fondant ball, mold a ghost shape and cut out triangle shapes from its base using a knife.

STEP 2

★ Mold two ears from 1½-inch (4 cm) orange fondant balls, one pointing up and the other down, and attach to the top of the ghost with edible glue.

★ Roll one small and one larger black fondant ball and attach to the ghost as eyes.

STEP 3

★ Allow to dry for at least 12 hours and place on a frosted cupcake.

Sleigh bells ring, are you listening?
Revel in these festive treats!

TOOLS AND MATERIALS

2¼-inch (5.5 cm) circle cutter

Black, yellow, red, white and green fondants

Knife or blade tool and rolling pin

Edible glue and brush

SANTA'S BELT

HOW TO MAKE

STEP 1

★ Cover a cupcake with flat, red fondant (see page 17).

★ Cut a 2¼-inch (5.5 cm) circle from rolled black fondant and cut it horizontally into three equal parts. Lay the center portion over the center of the cupcake to create Santa's belt.

STEP 2

★ Roll out some yellow fondant to ¼ inch (7 mm) thick and cut out a rectangle that is 1¾ x 1½ inches (4.5 x 4 cm). Using a knife, cut out a smaller rectangle to create the buckle. Apply to the top of the belt.

THE GIFT

HOW TO MAKE

STEP 1

★ Flat-frost a cupcake with white fondant (see page 17).

★ Roll out red fondant to ¼ inch (7 mm) thick and cut out three strips that are 3 x ½ inches (7.5 x 1.5 cm) and one strip that is 1 x ¼ inch (2.5cm x 7 mm). Apply one of the larger strips to the top of the cupcake as the ribbon.

★ Cut the second large strip in half widthwise and cut inverted triangles from one end of each piece to make two tails for the bow.

STEP 2

★ Fold the ends of the third strip into the center. Create the center of the bow by pinching the bow and applying the center strip, securing at the back with glue. Attach to the top of the ribbon with glue.

★ Assemble the bow and tails on the cupcake and glue into position.

THE SNOWMAN

HOW TO MAKE

STEP 1

★ Flat-frost a cupcake with white fondant (see page 17).

★ Roll out the red fondant to ¼ inch (7 mm) thick and cut out four 1 x ¼ inch (2.5 cm x 7 mm) strips. Repeat with the green fondant. Glue the strips together, alternating red and green.

STEP 2

★ After 30 minutes, when dry, cut out two scarf shapes and apply to the top of the cupcake with glue.

★ Roll three ¼-inch (7 mm) balls of black fondant to create the buttons. Apply to the cupcake with glue.

HOLIDAY WREATH

This festive cupcake wreath makes the perfect centerpiece to any holiday celebration!

TOOLS AND MATERIALS

Knife or blade tool and rolling pin

Red, green and brown fondants

Scissors

Holly leaf cutter

Flower forming cups

Disposable piping bag (end cut with an inverted "V")

Green frosting

Edible glue and brush

Red berry candies

Non-edible gold bells

Cake board

THE WREATH

HOW TO MAKE

STEP 1

★ Roll six ½-inch (1.5 cm) brown fondant balls and mold each one into a pinecone. Use scissors to cut the scales on each one. Leave to dry for 24 hours.

STEP 2

★ Roll out and cut out 12 holly leaves. Use a blade tool to mark the leaves and arrange on a forming cup. Glue the berry candies in place and leave to dry for 24 hours.

STEP 3

★ To make the bow, cut out two 1½ x 5-inch (4 x 12.5 cm) rectangles from red fondant, fold them over and support them using some paper towel. Pinch the ends together. Cut a 2 x ½-inch (5 x 1 cm) strip of red fondant and wrap it around the bow loop ends. Cut two 2½ x 1½-inch (6.5 x 4 cm) rectangles, cut away an inverted triangle from one end of each and pinch the other end together. Assemble the bow and leave to dry for 24 hours.

★ Assemble the cupcakes together in a ring on a cake board. You can use a little frosting on the bottom of each cupcake to fix them in place. Begin frosting with a random leaf pattern. When all the cupcakes are covered, place your dried bow, holly, pinecones and the bells on top of the cupcakes. Always make your guests aware of non-edible items.

ELVES AND STOCKINGS

Get ready for the holidays with Santa's little helpers and these adorable personalized Christmas stockings!

TOOLS AND MATERIALS

Knife or blade tool and rolling pin

1½-inch (4 cm) star cutter

Skin-colored fondant or almond paste

Green fondant

Hershey's Kisses

Edible glue and brush

Plastic wrap

THE ELVES

HOW TO MAKE

STEP 1

★ Roll out the green fondant to ⅛ inch (3 mm) thick and cut out the star shape.

★ Roll out ½-inch (1.5 cm) and ¼-inch (7 mm) balls of skin-colored fondant or almond paste.

STEP 2

★ Mark eyes and a mouth with the toothpick or indent the mouth with a piping tip. Add a small ball of fondant for the nose.

★ To make the ears, cut the smaller ball of fondant in two, re-roll into balls and place under plastic wrap. Flatten down to one side, remove the wrap and pinch the flattened side to a point. Glue the ears to the head.

STEP 3

★ Glue the head to the star collar and glue a Hershey's Kiss to the top of the head. Glue to the top of a flat-frosted mini cupcake.

TOOLS AND MATERIALS

Knife or blade tool and rolling pin

Red and white fondants

Toothpick and skewer

Black edible-ink pen

White edible glitter

Edible glue and brush

PERSONALIZED STOCKINGS

HOW TO MAKE

STEP 1

★ Roll out the red fondant to ⅛ inch (3 mm) thick and cut out the boot shape using the template on page 140. Also cut out a 3-inch (7.5 cm) long strip of red fondant for the ribbon.

★ Roll out the white fondant and cut out a rectangle that is 1 x ¾ inches (2.5 x 2cm) wide and cut the ends inward.

STEP 2

★ Glue the stocking and ribbon onto a green, flat fondant-covered cupcake and allow to dry for 12 hours.

STEP 3

★ Using a black edible-ink pen, write your required names on the stocking.

★ Sprinkle with white edible glitter.

FESTIVE TREE

Time for family and friends to gather around the tree! A fantastic cupcake display—perfect for a large holiday gathering!

TOOLS AND MATERIALS

50 regular sized cupcakes

12 mini-cupcakes

7-inch (17.5 cm) diameter x 15-inches (38 cm) high polystyrene craft cone

Toothpicks

8 ounces (225 g) red fondant

8 ounces (225 g) green fondant

2½-inch (5 cm) circle cutter

Edible glitter

Red or green tissue paper (optional)

Edible glue and brush

THE BAUBLE TREE

HOW TO MAKE

STEP 1

★ Cover your cupcakes with the green and red fondant, so they are flat (as shown on page 17).

STEP 2

★ If you don't want to see any white polystyrene on your finished tower, you can cover it in red or green tissue paper.

★ Start at the bottom of your cone and, using toothpicks half inserted into the polystyrene, position your cupcakes around the base of the cone, alternating between the green and red cupcakes.

★ When you have completed the first row, decide on what is the front and position the cupcakes on the second row so that they rest between the two cupcakes below. Go halfway around this time and continue up so that the front looks uniform.

★ Continue the pattern around the back of the cone. As you work your way around, you will find it harder to fit in the larger cupcakes so you can insert the mini-cupcakes into any gaps.

★ When you have finished fixing the cupcakes in place, make sure they are secure. You may need to use extra toothpicks on some cakes; these can be pushed through the side of the liner and into the cone.

★ To finish, sprinkle some edible glitter over the cupcakes and fix a star decoration to the top of your cone.

HYDRANGEA CENTERPIECE

This fabulous floral table centerpiece is sure to impress your guests! Perfect for a wedding table, where the flowers double as favors!

TOOLS AND MATERIALS

Rolling pin

White fondant

Hydrangea cutter and mold

Edible pearl luster spray

6-inch (15 cm) polystyrene craft ball

6-inch (15 cm) diameter vase

16 cupcakes baked in white liners

Floral tape or a hot glue gun

Piping bag with white frosting

Wilton 1M/2110 tip

Toothpicks

THE BLOSSOMS

HOW TO MAKE

STEP 1

★ Roll out the white fondant to 1/16 inch (2 mm) thick and, using the hydrangea cutter, cut out a single flower.

★ Now press it into the hydrangea mold to create the individual blossom. Repeat twice more and stand the blossoms against each other so that they dry in a three dimensional shape.

★ You will need 10 blossoms per cupcake. Allow them to dry for 24 hours and spray with pearl luster spray for a subtle shimmer finish.

STEP 2

★ Fix a 6-inch (15 cm) polystyrene craft ball into a suitably sized vase, either by taping or using a hot-glue gun.

★ Starting at the top and in the center, insert a toothpick to secure the first cupcake. Then work around and insert six more cupcakes and then a final ring around the bottom. You may need to apply additional toothpicks to secure any loose cupcakes.

STEP 3

★ Using a Wilton 1M/2110 tip, apply a swirl of white frosting to a cupcake while it is still attached. Immediately apply the 10 hydrangea blossoms, so they are glued to the cupcakes with the frosting.

★ Repeat so that the blossoms cover all the cupcakes. You can also add some extra blossoms to any obvious gaps between the cupcakes.

★ Make sure your guests remove the toothpicks before eating.

MINI ROSE BOUQUET

This beautiful bouquet of mini-cupcakes decorated with hand-piped roses is an elegant addition to the top of a wedding cake.

TOOLS AND MATERIALS

4-inch (10 cm) polystyrene craft ball

18 mini-cupcakes baked in silver liners

Toothpicks

Skewer

Pink frosting in a piping bag

Wilton no.104 rose tip

NOTES ON THE CAKE

A 7-inch (18 cm) round cake covered in white fondant was used, a pink satin ribbon wrapped around the middle and secured at the back with a pin. A pink satin ribbon bow at the front is secured with a diamanté brooch. Remember to remove any non-edible items before serving.

THE ROSES

HOW TO MAKE

STEP 1

★ Slice off the bottom from a 4-inch (10 cm) polystyrene craft ball two-thirds of the way down (a serrated bread knife is ideal for this job). Make a hole in the bottom at the center with a skewer—this will help to secure it to the cake at a later stage.

★ Starting at the top and in the center, insert a toothpick to secure the first cupcake. You may need to trim the toothpicks if they are too long. Now work your way around and insert six more cupcakes and then a final ring around the bottom (as shown).

STEP 2

★ Remove a cupcake and pipe a rose using pink frosting and a Wilton no.104 rose tip (see page 15). Replace on the bouquet, take the next cupcake and repeat the process.

★ You may need to secure any loose cupcakes with additional toothpicks.

STEP 3

★ Place the completed bouquet on top of a cake. It can be secured with either a blob of frosting or by placing a skewer in the cake and allowing the sharp end to protrude 2 inches (5 cm) out of the cake. Gently lower the bouquet onto the skewer, making sure it's centered.

★ Ensure that your guests remove the toothpicks before eating.

DAISY CUPCAKE TOWER

This cupcake tower is ideal for a wedding or large celebration. The daisies can be made in any color to match the theme.

TOOLS AND MATERIALS

1½-inch (4 cm) daisy flower cutter

6-inch (15 cm) round sponge cake covered in white fondant on a cake drum

4-inch (10 cm) round polystyrene dummy cake

White and yellow fondants

Toothpicks

3-feet (1 m) of 1-inch (2.5 cm) yellow satin ribbon

¼-inch (7 mm) circle cutter

Parchment paper

Edible glue and brush

THE DAISY CAKE

HOW TO MAKE

★ Cover a 6-inch (15 cm) round cake with white fondant (see page 16). Now cover the 4-inch (10 cm) polystyrene dummy cake with white fondant using the same technique. Allow the fondant to dry for 24 hours.

★ When the fondant is dry, insert four toothpicks halfway into the base of the polystyrene dummy cake; this will be the top tier. Position it centrally on top of the real cake and insert the toothpicks into the cake. Trim the base of each layer with a coordinating yellow satin ribbon and secure at the back with a pin. Remember to remove any pins before serving.

★ Roll out the yellow fondant and cut out lots of ¼-inch (7 mm) circles. Glue them to the top tier of the cake in a polka-dot pattern. If you are not confident doing this freehanded, print a polka-dot pattern from the Internet and lay it on the cake. Make a pin prick for each dot to guide you and glue the yellow fondant dots in place.

★ For the base tier, make nine fondant daisies in the same way as you did for the daisy cupcake toppers. Leave to dry for just five minutes and then, while they are still pliable, glue onto the side of the base layer.

★ An acrylic cupcake stand can be used to display the cake; this can be adjusted to fit the number of cupcakes required.

THE DAISY CUPCAKES

HOW TO MAKE

★ Roll out the white fondant to ⅛ inch (3 mm) thick and use a 1½-inch (4 cm) daisy cutter to cut out the petals. Take some yellow fondant, cut out a ¼-inch (7 mm) ball and glue it to the center of the daisy, pressing flat.

★ Using a palette knife, move the completed daisy to a flat surface covered in parchment paper. Allow to dry for 24 hours.

★ Once dry, place upright on a frosted cupcake baked in a coordinating yellow liner.

WEDDING CUPCAKES

These cupcake designs would complement any wedding with their classic colors and themes.

TOOLS AND MATERIALS

Knife or craft knife and rolling pin

White and black fondants

¼-inch (7 mm) flower cutter

Pearl ball sprinkles

Edible glue and brush

THE WEDDING CAKE

HOW TO MAKE

STEP 1

★ Roll out the white fondant to a thickness of ¼ inch (7 mm) and cut out a rectangle that is 2 x 1½ inches (5 x 4 cm).

★ Create a three-tier cake shape by cutting out smaller rectangles for each layer.

STEP 2

★ Roll out a small amount of black fondant to ⅛ inch (3 mm) thick and cut out ⅛-inch (3 mm) wide black strips to create the black ribbon around each layer of the cake.

★ Glue in place with edible glue.

STEP 3

★ Using a ¼-inch (7 mm) flower cutter, cut out two small flowers from the black fondant. In the center of each flower, glue a small pearl ball sprinkle or a small ball of white fondant.

★ Allow to dry for at least 24 hours and place on a frosted cupcake.

TOOLS AND MATERIALS

White, yellow, and green fondants

2-inch (5 cm) heart cutter

½-inch (1 cm) heart cutter

Cake decorating sponge

Paper towel

Edible glue and paintbrush

THE CALLA LILY

HOW TO MAKE

STEP 1

★ Roll out the white fondant to a thickness of ⅛ inch (3 mm), and cut out a 2-inch (5 cm) heart shape. Curl the top curves of the heart over each other and secure them with glue. Add a small roll of paper towel into the resulting funnel so that the flower can dry holding its shape. Leave to dry for 24 hours and then remove the paper towel.

STEP 2

★ Roll out a small amount of green fondant and cut out a ½-inch (1 cm) heart. Curl the green heart around the base of the white fondant flower to represent the leaf and glue in place.

★ Roll out a thin sausage of yellow fondant to form the spadix, and glue to the center of the flower. Place a small piece of paper towel underneath to provide support while the spadix is gluing. This can be removed after 24 hours.

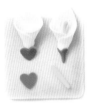

STEP 3

★ Once dry, place on top of a frosted cupcake.

TOOLS AND MATERIALS

Knife or craft knife and rolling pin

White and yellow fondants

2½-inch (6.5 cm) daisy or gerbera flower cutter

2½-inch (6.5 cm) diameter terra-cotta flowerpot (available at garden centers)

Edible glue and brush

THE DAISY FLOWERPOTS

HOW TO MAKE

STEP 1

★ Roll out the white fondant to a thickness of ¼ inch (7 mm) and leave for a few minutes to create a crust. This will help the fondant release from the flower cutter.

★ Using a 2½-inch (6.5 cm) daisy or gerber flower cutter, cut out the flower shape and place on parchment paper.

STEP 2

★ Take a ¼-inch (7 mm) ball of yellow fondant and flatten it with your finger to create the center of the flower.

★ Using a ball tool, indent the center of the flower and then, using a knife or blade tool, indent the outer ring of the flower's petals. Glue to the center of the flower.

STEP 3

★ Allow to dry. Insert the unfrosted cupcake into a 2½-inch (6.5 cm) diameter terra-cotta flowerpot (don't force it, you still need to get it out to eat!).

★ Frost the cupcake and, using a spatula, carefully pick up the daisy and place it onto the cupcake, facing forward.

TEMPLATES

Photocopy this page, cut out the template and place on the rolled fondant. Cut around the template with a craft knife.

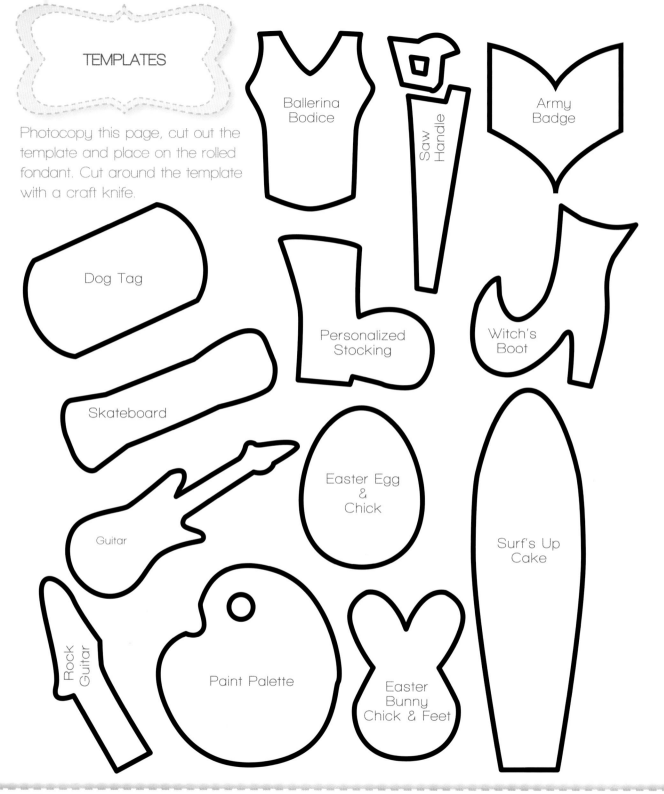

Ballerina Bodice

Saw Handle

Army Badge

Dog Tag

Personalized Stocking

Witch's Boot

Skateboard

Easter Egg & Chick

Surf's Up Cake

Guitar

Rock Guitar

Paint Palette

Easter Bunny Chick & Feet

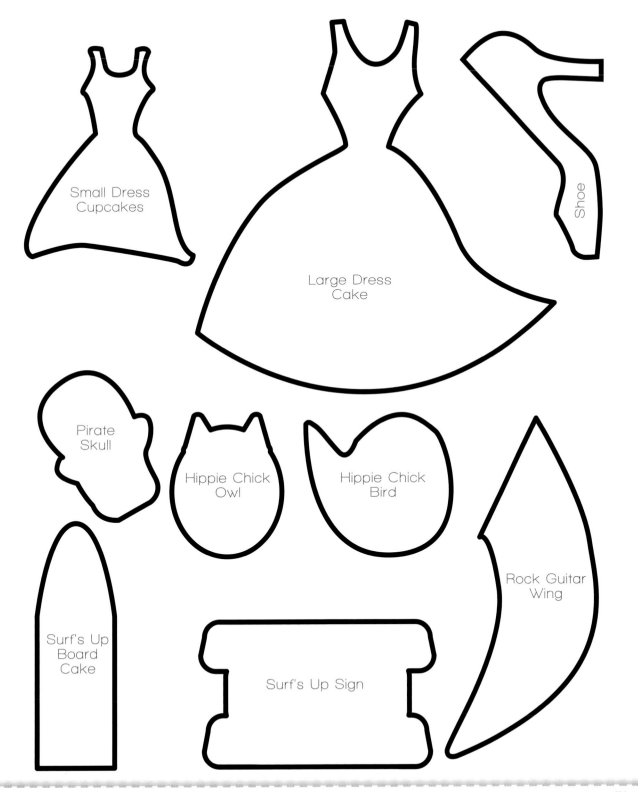

Small Dress
Cupcakes

Large Dress
Cake

Shoe

Pirate
Skull

Hippie Chick
Owl

Hippie Chick
Bird

Rock Guitar
Wing

Surf's Up
Board
Cake

Surf's Up Sign

Index

A

almond paste 21
Anchor 37
Apple 106
Apples and Crayons 115
Army Badge 65

B

Babes in Blanket 29
Baby Name Blocks 32–33
baking equipment 8
Ballerina 55
Bananas 109
Barn 50
Bird 77
Black Dress 101
Blossoms 133
Blush 56
Boat 35, 36
Bobo the Clown 44–45
Bridge 91
Bunny 121
Bushes 96
buttercream, coloring 14
Butterfly 76
Buttons the Bear 26–27

C

cake recipes 10–12
cakes
    Baby Name Blocks 32–33
    Bobo the Clown 44–45
    Buttons the Bear 26–27
    Daisy Cupcake Tower
        136–137
    Darcy, Dog in a Handbag
        58–59
    Farm 46–50
    Hippie Chick 74–77

Luau Dancer 103–105
Nautical Name Cake
    34–37
Pirate Treasure Island
    51–53
Princess 60–61
Rock Tattoo 70–71
Shopping 98–102
Southern-Fried Chicken
    88–89
Spotty Duck 30–31
Surf's Up! Radical Cakes
    82–85
Verity the Fairy 40–41
Calla Lily 138–139
Camouflage 64
candies 21
Chalkboard 114–115
Chicken 48, 49
Chicks 120–121
Christmas 124–131
Cocktail 117
Cola 78
coloring 14, 15, 17
Cool Dudes 68–69
Cory the Caterpillar 38
Cow 48
Cowboy Hat 63
cupcake ensembles
    Daisy Cupcake Tower
        136–137
    Festive Tree 130–131
    Fruit Basket 106–109
    Garden 94–97
    Golf Course 90–91
    Holiday Wreath 126–127
    Hydrangea Centerpiece
        132–133
    Mini Rose Bouquet
        134–135
    Pizza 88–89

Soccer Field 80–81
Sunflower Bouquet 110–111
cupcakes
    Army 64–65
    Baby Cakes 28–29
    Boys' Toys 42–43, 62–63
    Casino Night 116–117
    Celebrations 114
    Christmas 124–125,
        128–129
    Cool Dudes 68–69
    Cute Cupcake Toppers
        54–57
    DIY 92–93
    Easter 120–121
    Enchanted Garden 38–39
    Farm 46–50
    Halloween 122–123
    Hippie Chick 74–77
    Hobbies 112–113
    Movie Night 78–79
    Nautical Name Cake
        34–37
    Occasions 113
    Pirate Treasure Island 53
    Quirky Characters 66–67
    Red, White and Blue Stars
        118–119
    Shopping 102
    Surfboard 84–85
    Thank Yous 114–115
    Wedding Cupcakes
        138–139

D

Daisy Cupcake Tower
    136–137
Daisy Flowerpot 139
Darcy, Dog in a Handbag
    58–59

decorating tools 9
decorations 20–23
Dewdrop 57
Dice 116
Digger 42
Dirt 91
DIY 92–93
Dog Tags 64–65
Dress 102
Drumsticks 88–89
Duck 48, 49, 91

E

edible decorations 22
edible-ink pens 22
edible paints 22
Eggs 120
Elves 128
Enchanted Garden 38–39
equipment 8–9

F

Farm 46–50
Feather Headdress 62–63
Festive Tree 130–131
Fire Engine 43
Flags 36, 119
Flip-flops 84
Flowerpots 96
fondant 13
    coloring 17
    covering cake 16
    cutters 19
    decorations 20
    drying 19
    flat-fondant cupcake 17
    frilling 19
    modeling 18
    preparing cake for
        fondant 13

templates 18, 140–141
Football Player 62
frosting 13, 14–15, 17
Fruit Basket 106–109

G

Garden 94–97
Garden Tools 97
Ghost 123
glitters 22
Gold Booty 53
Golf Course 90–91
Grapes 109
Green Peppers 89
Greens 90
Guitar 71
gum paste 20

H

Ham 89
Hammer 92
Hamster 54
Hatbox 101
Heart 76
Hippie Chick 74–77
Holiday Wreath 126–127
Horse 47
Hosepipe 95
Hot dog 78–79
Hydrangea Centerpiece 132–133

J

Justin, the Hipster 68–69

L

Lighthouse 35, 37
Lightning Man 67
Luau Dancer 103–105
luster spray 22

M

Marshmallow Popcorn 79
marzipan 21
Masks 113
Mushrooms 88

N

Nautical Flags 36, 119
Nautical Name Cake 34–35
New Home 114
non-edible decorations 23
nonpareils 21

O

Olives 89
Orange 108
Owl 75

P

paint 22
Palette 112
Peace Sign 77
Pear 108
Pepperoni 88
Pig 47
Pineapple 89
piping effects 21
    grass effect 15
    hair effect 15
    hand-piped roses 15
Pirate Treasure Island 51–53
Pizza 88–89
Poker Chips 116–117
Polynesian Flower 105
Pony 54–55
Princess 60–61

Q

Quirky Characters 66–67

R

Rock Guitar 69
Rock Tattoo 70–71
Rose 71
Rose Bouquet 134–135
Rosette 118
Royston the Monster 66
Rubber Boots 96

S

Sally the Snail 39
Santa's Belt 124
Saw 93
Sewing Kit 112–113
Shark Bite 66–67
Sheep 49
Shoe 102
Shoebox 100
Shopping 98–102
Shopping Bag 98–99
Sign 84
Skateboard 68
Skull and Crossbones 53
Snowman 125
Soccer Field 80–81
Southern-Fried Chicken 88–89
Spotty Duck 30–31

sprinkles 21
Stepping Stones 95
Stockings 129
Stroller 28
Sunflower Bouquet 110–111
Surf's Up! Radical Cakes
    82–85
Surfboard 82–83, 84–85

T

Tape Measure 92–93
Tractor 42–43
Treasure Chest 52
Trees 90, 96
Triple Star 118–119
Twinkle 56–57

V

Verity the Fairy 40–41

W

Watering Can 94
Weather Vane 50
Wedding Cake 138
Winged Heart 70–71
Witch's Hat 122
Witch's Legs 122–123

Suppliers

You can purchase a whole range of equipment and materials, including fondant and cutters, from the following online suppliers.

UNITED STATES AND CANADA

Formaggio Kitchen
formaggiokitchen.com
Shop online

N.Y. Cake
nycake.com
Shop online

Flour Confections
flourconfections.ca
Shop online

Satin Ice Rolled Fondant
rolledfondant.com
Shop online

Vanilla Sky Ingredients
vanillaskyingredientscompany.com
Shop online

Kerekes
bakedeco.com
Shop online

Cake Mischief
cakemischief.com
Shop online

Golda's Kitchen
goldaskitchen.com
Shop online

Goodies Cake Decorating & Candy Making Supplies
goodiescakesupplies.com
Shop online

Credits

All photographs and illustrations are the copyright of Quintet Publishing Ltd While every effort has been made to credit contributors, Quintet would like to apologize should there have been any omissions or errors—and would be pleased to make the appropriate correction for future editions.